THE AUSTRALIAN
Women's Weekly

THE ESSENTIAL VEGAN

THE AUSTRALIAN
Women's Weekly

THE ESSENTIAL VEGAN

CONTENTS

LET'S TALK VEGAN

Welcome to *The Essential Vegan* cookbook. Whether you're a long-time vegan or a newbie to this way of eating, you've picked up the right book!

There are a number of reasons why people choose to embrace a vegan diet, ranging from concern for animal welfare, to environmental and health reasons. Did you know that those on a vegan diet tend to have a lower risk of developing type-2 diabetes, heart disease and also some cancers compared to their omniverous counterparts? It's because a well-balanced plant-based diet includes a wide array of plant matter, fibre and tends to be low fat.

Be aware though, as with any diet it's possible to make poor choices such as eating too much fat or sugar.

If you're vegan, you'll also have to take care to ensure your body is getting enough vitamin B12, calcium, iodine, iron, zinc and omega-3 fatty acids. Learn which foods include these nutrients and make sure to include them as part of a balanced diet.

As you'd know, a vegan diet is wholly plant-based and excludes all animal products. In addition to the obvious, foods like honey and gelatine are also off limits. Never fear though, there's a massive range of foods still available to you including many commonly used ingredients you probably already have in your kitchen.

Continuing your vegan way of life or making the leap from vegetarianism to veganism (or directly to veganism) is made flavourful and fun with *The Essential Vegan*. You can choose from an expansive collection of recipes, from falafel bowls to kimchi to tofu burgers and even a 'shepherdless' pie, all using common ingredients as well as, in some cases, readily-available vegan substitutes like cheddar-style cheese, egg-replacer and plant-based mince.

It's not all vegan substitutes though! We've broken this book down into hero food groups that will help you achieve a nutritionally balanced vegan diet. You've got Power Pulses where you'll find recipes featuring beans and lentils; Great Grains with recipes incorporating rice, grains and noodles; Orange Vegies showcasing the versatility of sweet potato and pumpkin; All in the Family (cauliflower, broccoli, green veg); Meet Your Protein (tofu, nuts and seeds, plant-based mince) and Magic Mushrooms! It makes picking your meal a breeze, since you can search according to ingredients you have on hand (or by what you're craving!).

So open up your pantry or fridge, choose your ingredient, then flip to the corresponding section of *The Essential Vegan* to find a recipe that sings to you.

DISCLAIMER While every care has been taken in creating the recipes in this book to ensure they are vegan, care must be taken when purchasing ingredients, especially those manufactured such as sauces, condiments and packaged foods. Always check the ingredient label to ensure products you buy are vegan. The publisher will not be held liable for any action or claim resulting from the use of this book. Please note, though there is evidence that eating a predominantly plant-based diet is healthy, it is not suitable for children.

LABEL CHECK!
AVOID PRODUCTS THAT LIST ANY OF THE FOLLOWING ON THEIR LABEL: CASEIN, WHEY, LACTALBUMIN, LACTULOSE, ISINGLASS, TALLOW, GELATINE, ALBUMIN.
INCREASE YOUR BODY'S UPTAKE OF IRON SIXFOLD BY COMBINING YOUR IRON SOURCE WITH VITAMIN C RICH FOODS.
VITAMIN B12 IS ONLY FOUND IN MEAT, SO BE ON THE LOOK OUT FOR VITAMIN B12 FORTIFIED FOODS, OR TAKE A SUPPLEMENT.

PROTEIN-RICH & INEXPENSIVE

POWER PULSES

BEANS • LENTILS Pulses have so much to recommend on any diet. Their ease of use and lack of expense, plus abundant protein, fibre, iron and array of B vitamins and minerals mean they are both your ally in the kitchen and key to meeting your nutritional needs on a vegan diet. We have plenty of recipe inspiration for everything from speedy lunch bowls to satisfying dinners.

LOADED CHICKPEA MASALA WITH CHAPATIS

- 1 tbsp olive oil
- 1 large onion (200g), sliced thinly
- 1 clove garlic, crushed
- 1 tbsp finely chopped fresh ginger
- 2 tsp yellow mustard seeds
- 2 tsp garam masala
- 1 tsp ground coriander
- ½ tsp ground turmeric
- ¼ tsp cayenne pepper
- 400g (12½oz) can diced tomatoes
- ⅔ cup (160ml) canned light coconut milk
- 1 small cauliflower (1kg), cut into florets
- 400g (12½oz) can chickpeas (garbanzo beans), drained, rinsed
- 1 bunch silverbeet (swiss chard) (750g), stems removed, leaves chopped coarsely
- ⅓ cup (95g) non-dairy yoghurt
- ¼ cup coriander (cilantro) sprigs
- wholemeal chapatis, to serve

1 Heat olive oil in a large saucepan over medium-high heat. Add onion; cook, stirring, for 5 minutes or until soft. Add garlic and ginger; cook, stirring, for 1 minute or until fragrant. Add mustard seeds; once they start popping, add remaining spices and stir for 1 minute or until fragrant.

2 Add tomatoes, coconut milk and ⅓ cup (80ml) water to pan; bring to the boil. Add cauliflower and chickpeas; return to the boil. Reduce heat to low-medium; cook, covered, for 15 minutes or until cauliflower is tender.

3 Stir silverbeet through chickpea mixture; simmer for 3 minutes or until wilted.

4 Serve chickpea masala topped with non-dairy yoghurt and coriander sprigs; accompany with chapatis.

PREP + COOK TIME 40 minutes **SERVES** 4

HIGH IN PROTEIN

SUPER
SPEEDY

FAST FABULOUS FALAFEL BOWL

- 1¼ cups (200g) coarse burghul
- 450g (14½oz) packaged ready-made falafels
- 2 lebanese cucumbers (260g), seeded, chopped finely
- 2 green onions (scallions), sliced thinly
- 1 cup mint leaves
- ¼ cup (60ml) olive oil
- 2 tbsp white wine vinegar
- 1 oak leaf lettuce, leaves separated
- 200g (6½oz) store-bought baba ganoush
- 2 small pocket pitta (160g), halved, to serve

1 Place burghul and 1¼ cups (310ml) boiling water in a large heatproof bowl. Stand for 15 minutes or until water is absorbed and burghul is tender.
2 Meanwhile, heat falafels according to packet directions.
3 Add cucumber, green onion, mint, oil and vinegar to burghul; toss gently to combine. Season to taste.
4 Place burghul mixture and lettuce in a large bowl or platter; top with baba ganoush and falafels. Serve with warmed pitta.

PREP + COOK TIME 30 minutes **SERVES** 4

SWAP You can use home-made or store-bought hummus instead of the baba ganoush, if you like.

EGGPLANT & CHICKPEA TART

extra virgin olive oil spray
1 medium eggplant (300g), cut into 2cm (¾in) pieces
1 large red onion (300g), cut into thin wedges
300g (9½oz) five-spice firm tofu, cut into 4cm (1½in) pieces
3 tsp ground cumin
1½ tbsp extra virgin olive oil
300g (9½oz) non-dairy yoghurt
½ cup mint leaves, chopped finely
60g (2oz) baby rocket (arugula)
⅓ cup (50g) pomegranate seeds

CHICKPEA PASTRY

400g (12½oz) can chickpeas (garbanzo beans), drained, rinsed
1 cup (40g) Corn Flakes
½ cup (40g) quinoa flakes
2 tbsp linseed (flaxseed) meal

1 Preheat oven to 200°C/400°F. Spray a 23cm (9¼in) loose-based, fluted tart tin with oil spray.

2 To make chickpea pastry, pulse all ingredients with ¼ cup (60ml) water in a food processor until a soft dough forms. Using slightly damp hands, press dough evenly into the base and side of tin.

3 Line a large baking tray with baking paper. In a large bowl combine the eggplant, onion, tofu, cumin and oil; toss gently to combine, season with pepper. Spread onto lined tray; place on top shelf of oven. Place tart case on bottom shelf. Bake for 40 minutes, or until tart shell is crisp and eggplant and onion are golden and soft, turning eggplant halfway through cooking time. Cool to room temperature. (The tart shell will shrink during cooking and cooling.)

4 Meanwhile, combine non-dairy yoghurt and mint in a small bowl; season with pepper.

5 Spread cooled tart base evenly with yoghurt mixture; top with combined eggplant mixture and rocket. Sprinkle with pomegranate seeds.

PREP + COOK TIME 1 hour (+ cooling) **SERVES** 6

HIGH IN FIBRE

KIDNEY BEAN & VEGIE PATCH PIES

1 large orange sweet potato (500g)
5 flat mushrooms (400g)
1 medium eggplant (300g)
2 tbsp extra virgin olive oil
1 tsp ground cumin
1 tsp paprika
400g (12½oz) can black beans, drained, rinsed
400g (12½oz) can red kidney beans, drained, rinsed
560g (1lb) jar tomato pasta sauce

PIE TOPPING

1 wholemeal pitta bread pocket (150g)
½ cup (45g) rolled oats
½ cup (50g) walnuts
¼ cup (60ml) extra virgin olive oil
⅓ cup (25g) grated vegan parmesan-style cheese
1½ tbsp thyme leaves

1 Preheat oven to 220°C/425°F. Line two large oven trays with baking paper.
2 Cut sweet potato into 2.5cm (1in) pieces. Cut the mushrooms and eggplant into 2cm (¾in) pieces. Toss vegetables with oil and spices in a bowl; season well. Arrange in a single layer over prepared trays. Roast for 30 minutes or until soft and golden brown, swapping trays between shelves halfway through cooking time.
3 Meanwhile, make pie topping.
4 Combine beans, pasta sauce and 2 tablespoons water in a large heatproof bowl. Add hot cooked vegetables; stir to combine then season to taste. Divide mixture evenly among four 2-cup (500ml) ovenproof dishes. Divide pie topping among dishes.
5 Bake for 20 minutes or until top is golden and filling is bubbling. Serve topped with remaining thyme leaves.

PIE TOPPING Tear pitta coarsely then process with half the oats, half the walnuts and the oil until coarsely chopped and combined. Stir through the grated vegan parmesan, 1 tablespoon thyme leaves and the remaining oats and walnuts.

PREP + COOK TIME 1 hour 15 minutes **SERVES** 4

BLACK BEAN CHILLI WITH GUACAMOLE & CORN 'CHIPS'

olive-oil spray

1 large red onion (300g), chopped finely

1 medium red capsicum (bell pepper) (200g), seeded, chopped finely

1 large carrot (180g), chopped finely

3 celery stalks (450g), trimmed, chopped finely

2 cloves garlic, crushed

2 tsp ground cumin

2 tsp mexican chilli powder

1 tsp smoked paprika

1 tsp dried oregano

1 tbsp tomato paste

400g (12½oz) can diced tomatoes

400g (12½oz) can black beans, drained, rinsed

3 slices corn mountain bread (75g), cut into 36 triangles (see tip)

½ cup (140g) non-dairy yoghurt

⅓ cup (40g) grated vegan cheddar-style cheese

½ cup coriander (cilantro) leaves

lime wedges, to serve

GUACAMOLE

1 small avocado (200g), chopped

¼ cup (70g) non-dairy yoghurt

3 tsp lime juice

1 Spray a large heavy-based saucepan with oil; heat over medium heat. Add onion, capsicum, carrot and celery; cook, stirring, for 5 minutes or until onion softens.

2 Add garlic, spices and oregano to pan; cook, stirring, for 1 minute. Add tomato paste; cook, stirring, for a further minute. Add canned tomatoes, black beans and 1 cup (250ml) water; bring to the boil. Reduce heat to low; cook, covered, stirring occasionally, for 20 minutes or until vegetables soften.

3 Meanwhile, preheat oven to 200°C/400°F.

4 To make guacamole, mash ingredients in a small bowl until smooth.

5 Place mountain bread triangles on an oven tray. Place in oven for 5 minutes or until light golden and crisp.

6 Evenly divide black bean chilli, corn 'chips', guacamole, non-dairy yoghurt and vegan cheese among four bowls; sprinkle with coriander and season with pepper. Serve with lime wedges.

PREP + COOK TIME 40 minutes **SERVES** 4

TIP Making your own corn 'chips' from corn mountain bread makes this a healthier option than using regular corn chips.

HIGH IN IRON

SUPER
SPEEDY

INDIAN-ROASTED CHILLI, TOMATO & CHICKPEAS

- 400g (12½oz) can chickpeas (garbanzo beans), drained, rinsed
- 6 fresh long red chillies
- 1½ tsp brown mustard seeds
- 2 tsp cumin seeds
- ½ tsp chilli flakes
- 2 tsp ground turmeric
- ⅓ cup (80ml) extra virgin olive oil
- ¼ cup curry leaves, plus 3 extra sprigs
- 500g (1lb) ripe cherry truss tomatoes, cut into clusters
- 8 pappadums
- ½ cup (140g) non-dairy yoghurt

1 Preheat oven to 200°C/400°F. Line a large oven tray with baking paper.

2 Line another large tray with a clean tea towel. Spread chickpeas on towel to absorb excess moisture.

3 Cut the chillies in half lengthways, keeping the stalk attached; remove and discard seeds. Combine mustard and cumin seeds, chilli flakes, turmeric, oil and curry leaves in a large bowl. Add chillies, chickpeas and tomatoes. Season; toss gently to combine.

4 Spread mixture out over prepared oven tray. Top with the extra curry leaf sprigs. Bake, turning occasionally, for 15 minutes or until tomatoes have collapsed and chillies are tender.

5 Meanwhile, cook the pappadums according to packet directions.

6 Swirl a little of the tomato cooking juices through the non-dairy yoghurt. Serve chickpea mixture with yoghurt sauce and pappadums.

PREP + COOK TIME 30 minutes
SERVES 2 (or 4 as a side)

PERSIAN-STYLE LENTIL & CARROT SALAD

- 1 bunch mixed heirloom baby carrots (400g), trimmed, peeled
- 400g (12½oz) can chickpeas (garbanzo beans), drained, rinsed
- 400g (12½oz) can brown lentils, drained, rinsed
- 1 small red onion (100g), halved, sliced thinly
- 400g (12½oz) tomato medley, halved and quartered, depending on size
- 1 large pomegranate (430g), seeds removed
- 1 cup flat-leaf parsley leaves, chopped coarsely
- 200g (6½oz) vegan fetta-style cheese, drained
- lemon wedges, to serve

POMEGRANATE DRESSING

- ¼ cup (60ml) extra virgin olive oil
- 1 tbsp pomegranate molasses
- 1 tbsp lemon juice

1 Using a mandoline, V-slicer or wide vegetable peeler, shave carrots into 2mm-thick slices.

2 To make pomegranate dressing, place ingredients in a screw-top jar; shake well to combine. Season to taste.

3 Combine carrot, chickpeas, lentils, onion, tomatoes, pomegranate seeds and parsley in a large bowl; season to taste. Add dressing and toss to combine.

4 Top salad with crumbled vegan fetta and serve with lemon wedges.

PREP TIME 20 minutes **SERVES** 4

SUPER SPEEDY

LENTIL SAUSAGE ROLLS

2 x 400g (12½oz) cans lentils, drained, rinsed

1 small onion (80g), grated finely

2 cloves garlic, crushed

⅓ cup (45g) chopped roasted pistachios

1 tsp sweet paprika

1 tsp ground cumin

¼ tsp ground cinnamon

¼ tsp chilli flakes

10 sheets fillo pastry

cooking oil spray

¼ tsp sumac

dipping sauce of choice, to serve

1 Preheat oven to 200°C/400°F. Line an oven tray with baking paper.
2 Place lentils in a bowl; mash lightly with a fork. Add onion, garlic, pistachios, spices and chilli flakes; stir to combine. Season.
3 Layer five sheets of fillo pastry on a clean work bench, spraying each sheet with oil. Place half the lentil mixture along one long side of fillo; roll to enclose filling. Cut into four even lengths; place on lined tray. Repeat with remaining fillo and lentil mixture to make 8 rolls in total. Spray rolls with oil, then sprinkle with sumac.
4 Bake the lentil sausage rolls for 30 minutes or until golden. Serve rolls with your favourite dipping sauce.

PREP + COOK TIME 45 minutes **MAKES** 8

CURRIED LENTIL SOUP WITH ROAST PUMPKIN SEEDS

- ½ bunch coriander (cilantro)
- 1 tbsp extra virgin olive oil
- 1 medium onion (150g), chopped finely
- 2 cloves garlic, crushed
- 1 long red chilli, seeded, chopped finely
- 4cm (1½in) piece fresh ginger, grated finely
- 2 tsp grated fresh turmeric
- 1 tsp ground cumin
- 1 tsp garam masala
- 2 bay leaves
- 1 cup (150g) red lentils
- 300g (9½oz) kent pumpkin, cut into 2cm (¾in) cubes
- 4 medium tomatoes (600g), seeded, chopped finely
- 1 litre (4 cups) vegetable stock
- 1½ cups shredded curly kale
- 80g (2½oz) rye bread
- 2 tbsp pepitas (pumpkin seed kernels)
- ½ cup (140g) non-dairy yoghurt

1 Separate coriander roots, stems and leaves. Wash and finely chop roots and stems (reserve coriander leaves for another use).

2 Heat oil in a large heavy-based saucepan over medium heat. Add chopped coriander, onion, garlic, chilli and ginger; cook, stirring, for 4 minutes or until softened. Add turmeric, cumin, garam masala and bay leaves; cook, stirring, for 1 minute or until fragrant.

3 Add lentils, pumpkin, tomato, stock and 2 cups (500ml) water to pan; bring to the boil. Reduce heat to low; cook, covered, for 25 minutes or until lentils and pumpkin are very tender. Remove lid; cook for a further 10 minutes or until thickened, adding kale for the last 2 minutes of cooking time to wilt.

4 Meanwhile, preheat oven to 180°C/350°F. Grease and line two large oven trays.

5 Tear bread into small pieces. Spread over one tray; spread pepitas over second tray. Bake, stirring once halfway through cooking time, for 10 minutes or until bread is toasted.

6 Divide soup among bowls; top with rye croûtons, non-dairy yoghurt and pepitas.

PREP + COOK TIME 1 hour **SERVES** 4

LENTIL & FENNEL STUFFED TOMATOES

8 large vine-ripened tomatoes (1.75kg)
1 medium fennel bulb (300g), trimmed, fronds reserved
400g (12½oz) can brown lentils, drained, rinsed
2 cloves garlic, crushed
¼ cup dill, chopped finely
1 tsp ground cumin
1 tsp dried mint
½ cup (50g) coarsely chopped roasted walnuts
200g (6½oz) vegan fetta-style cheese, cut into 3cm (1¼in) pieces
2 tbsp extra virgin olive oil
1 tsp finely grated lemon rind

1 Preheat oven to 220°C/425°F. Line an oven tray with baking paper.

2 Slice tops off tomatoes; reserve. Using a small spoon, scoop out the flesh from each tomato; reserve ¼ cup tomato pulp. Place tomatoes on prepared tray.

3 Trim ⅓ cup fronds from fennel; reserve. Chop the remaining fronds. Slice fennel stalks into rounds and cut bulb into wedges. Combine lentils, garlic, dill, chopped fennel fronds, cumin, mint, walnuts and tomato pulp in a bowl. Mix well; season.

4 Spoon lentil mixture into each tomato cavity, pressing down firmly; cover with the tomato tops. Place fennel rounds and wedges and the vegan fetta on tray between the tomatoes. Drizzle with half the oil; season. Cook for 15 minutes or until tomatoes are tender.

5 Remove tomatoes from tray; cover to keep warm. Continue to cook the fennel and fetta for a further 15 minutes or until golden brown. Return tomatoes to tray; scatter with rind and reserved fennel fronds. Drizzle with remaining oil.

PREP + COOK TIME 40 minutes **SERVES** 4

MISO & LENTIL MOUSSAKA

- 120g (4oz) baby spinach leaves
- 2 cups (560g) non-dairy yoghurt
- 1 cup (80g) grated vegan parmesan-style cheese
- ⅓ cup (80ml) extra virgin olive oil
- 1 medium eggplant (300g), cut into 5mm (¼in) rounds
- 1 small orange sweet potato (250g), cut into 3mm (⅛in) rounds
- 1 small leek (200g), sliced thinly
- ¼ cup (60g) dashi miso soybean paste
- 2 cloves garlic, crushed
- 1 tsp ground allspice
- 400g (12½oz) can brown lentils, drained, rinsed
- 2 x 400g (12½oz) cans cherry tomatoes
- ¼ cup oregano leaves

1 Preheat oven to 180°C/350°F.

2 Place spinach in a heatproof bowl; cover with boiling water. Stand until just wilted; drain. Cool under cold running water. Using hands, squeeze out excess water. Blend or process spinach, non-dairy yoghurt and vegan parmesan until smooth; season to taste.

3 Heat 2 tablespoons of the oil in a large non-stick frying pan over high heat; cook eggplant, in batches, turning, for 2 minutes or until golden and almost tender. Remove from pan.

4 Heat 1 tablespoon oil in same pan over medium-high heat; cook sweet potato, in batches, turning, for 1 minute or until golden and almost tender. Remove from pan.

5 Heat remaining oil in same pan; cook leek, stirring, for 2 minutes or until softened. Add miso paste, garlic and allspice; cook for 2 minutes or until paste is thick. Add lentils and tomatoes; bring to the boil. Remove pan from heat; season to taste.

6 Divide the lentil mixture into four 2-cup (500ml) ovenproof dishes. Arrange eggplant rounds over lentils; top with yoghurt mixture, then sweet potato. Scatter with oregano; season with pepper.

7 Bake moussaka for 25 minutes or until golden and edges are crisp.

PREP + COOK TIME 1 hour **SERVES** 4

SMOKY RED LENTIL MEAT-LESS LOAF

You will need to soak the lentils 8 hours ahead.

- 1¼ cups (250g) dried red lentils
- 2 tbsp extra virgin olive oil
- 1 medium onion (150g), chopped finely
- 2 cloves garlic, chopped finely
- ¼ cup oregano leaves, chopped finely
- 1 tsp smoked paprika
- 1 medium carrot (120g)
- 2 medium parsnips (500g)
- ¾ cup (180ml) vegetable stock
- 3 tsp vegan egg replacer
- 1½ cups (180g) grated vegan cheddar-style cheese
- 120g (4oz) mixed salad leaves
- 1 cup (275g) tomato and smoky chipotle relish

1 Place lentils in a large bowl, cover with cold water; stand for 8 hours or overnight. Drain; rinse under cold water, drain well.

2 Preheat oven to 200°C/400°F. Oil a 13cm x 23cm (5¼in x 9¼in), 6cm (2½in) deep loaf pan; line base and sides with baking paper.

3 Heat oil in a medium frying pan over medium heat. Cook onion, garlic and oregano, stirring occasionally, for 5 minutes or until softened. Stir in paprika.

4 Meanwhile, scrub carrot and parsnips; leave unpeeled. Thinly slice half of one parsnip lengthways. Coarsely grate remaining parsnips and carrot. Combine stock and egg replacer in a large bowl. Stir in grated vegetables, 1¼ cups vegan cheddar, the lentils and onion mixture; season. Spoon mixture into prepared pan; spread and level with the back of a spoon. Top with sliced parsnip and remaining vegan cheddar. Cover with greased foil. Scrunch foil around sides of pan to secure.

5 Bake loaf for 30 minutes. Remove foil; bake for a further 30 minutes or until golden.

6 Stand loaf in pan for 5 minutes before turning, top-side up, onto a board. Cool for 15 minutes before slicing. Serve slices with salad leaves and relish.

PREP + COOK TIME 1 hour 20 minutes (+ standing & cooling)
SERVES 4

TIP You can pan-fry slices of the lentil loaf to serve in a burger bun as a vegan burger patty.

USED IN HEAPS OF CUISINES

GREAT GRAINS

RICE & GRAINS • NOODLES Whole grains are a fantastic source of complex carbs and they form the basis of many classic recipes. What would paella, biryani or congee be without rice? Aside from the familiar, you'll also find recipes for soba (buckwheat) noodles, barley and quinoa (we know that strictly speaking, protein-rich quinoa is a seed, but it cooks like a grain). Whatever grain you pick there's goodness to be gained.

VEGETABLE & OLIVE PAELLA

- 3 cups (750ml) vegetable stock
- pinch saffron threads
- 1 tbsp extra virgin olive oil
- 2 lebanese eggplants (200g), halved lengthways, quartered crossways
- 1 medium red onion (170g), chopped finely
- 2 cloves garlic, crushed
- 2 medium tomatoes (300g), seeded, chopped finely
- 1 small red capsicum (bell pepper) (150g), sliced thinly
- 2 tsp smoked paprika
- 1¾ cups (350g) arborio rice
- 1 cup (120g) frozen peas
- 100g (3oz) green beans, trimmed, halved lengthways
- ½ cup (60g) pitted kalamata olives
- ¼ cup flat-leaf parsley leaves, chopped

1 Place vegetable stock and 2 cups (500ml) water in a medium saucepan; bring to the boil. Remove from heat; stir in saffron.

2 Heat oil in a large frying pan over medium-high heat; cook eggplant, stirring occasionally, for 5 minutes or until browned. Remove from pan.

3 Add onion and garlic to same pan with tomato, capsicum and paprika; cook, stirring, until onion softens. Add rice; stir to coat in mixture. Stir in stock mixture; bring to the boil. Reduce heat; simmer for 20 minutes or until rice is almost tender.

4 Arrange eggplant, peas and beans evenly on paella; cook, covered, for 10 minutes or until beans and rice are tender. Season. Top with olives; stand, covered, for 5 minutes. Just before serving, sprinkle with parsley.

PREP + COOK TIME 1 hour 15 minutes **SERVES** 4

SPICED VEGIE BIRYANI

- 2 medium onions (300g)
- 1 tbsp vegetable oil
- 1 clove garlic, crushed
- 2 tsp garam masala
- 400g (12½oz) can diced tomatoes
- 1 medium potato (200g), cut into 1cm (½in) pieces
- 1 medium red capsicum (bell pepper) (200g), cut into 2cm (¾in) pieces
- 1½ cups (300g) basmati rice
- 8 cardamom pods, bruised
- ½ tsp chilli powder
- ¼ tsp ground turmeric
- ¼ cup (40g) sultanas
- 1 lebanese cucumber (130g), peeled into ribbons (see tip)
- 1 medium carrot (120g), peeled into ribbons (see tip)
- ¼ cup (20g) roasted flaked natural almonds
- ⅓ cup coriander (cilantro) sprigs
- ⅓ cup small mint leaves

1 Thinly slice 1 onion; finely chop remaining onion. Keep separate.

2 Heat half the oil in a large saucepan over medium-high heat; cook garlic and sliced onion, stirring, for 5 minutes or until onion softens. Add garam masala; cook, stirring, for 1 minute. Stir in tomatoes, potato and ½ cup (125ml) water; bring to the boil. Reduce heat; simmer, covered, for 10 minutes. Add capsicum; simmer, covered, for another 10 minutes or until vegetables are tender.

3 Meanwhile, heat remaining oil in a medium saucepan over medium-high heat; cook chopped onion, stirring, for 4 minutes or until soft. Add rice and spices; cook, stirring, for 1 minute or until fragrant. Stir in the sultanas and 1½ cups (375ml) water; bring to the boil. Reduce heat to low; simmer, covered, for 15 minutes or until rice is just tender and water is absorbed.

4 Divide rice and vegetable mixtures among bowls; top with cucumber, carrot, almonds and herbs.

PREP + COOK TIME 45 minutes **SERVES** 4

TIP To peel cucumber and carrot into ribbons, use a wide vegetable peeler.

BROWN RICE CONGEE WITH TOFU

- 6 cloves garlic
- 2 cups (500ml) vegetable stock
- 1½ cups (300g) brown rice
- 2 tbsp finely chopped fresh ginger
- 1 green onion (scallion), sliced thinly
- ½ cup (125ml) vegetable oil
- 200g (6½oz) firm marinated tofu, cut into 2cm (¾in) thick slices
- 2 tbsp tamari
- 2 tsp sesame seeds, toasted
- ⅓ cup coriander (cilantro) leaves

1 Finely chop 1 garlic clove; thinly slice remaining cloves.
2 Place stock, rice, chopped garlic, ginger, green onion and 1.75 litres (7 cups) water in a large saucepan; bring to the boil. Reduce heat to low; simmer, partially covered, for 1½ hours or until rice breaks down and forms a thick porridge-like consistency.
3 Heat oil in a small saucepan over medium heat; cook sliced garlic for 1 minute or until golden. Remove garlic with a slotted spoon; drain on paper towel. Reserve oil to serve.
4 Add tofu slices and tamari to rice mixture; stir over heat until hot. Ladle the congee into bowls; drizzle with reserved garlic oil and top with fried garlic, sesame seeds and coriander.

PREP + COOK TIME 2 hours **SERVES** 6

TIP If you like, stir 2 tablespoons sriracha into the reserved garlic oil before serving.

GOOD FOR
ENERGY

QUINOA FALAFEL WITH BEETROOT HUMMUS

- 400g (12½oz) can chickpeas (garbanzo beans), drained, rinsed
- ½ cup (40g) quinoa flakes
- 2 tsp ground cumin
- 2 tsp ground coriander
- 4 green onions (scallions), chopped
- 1 long green chilli, chopped
- ½ cup finely chopped coriander (cilantro) leaves and stems, plus extra leaves to serve
- 1 tbsp golden linseed (flaxseed) meal
- ¼ cup (60ml) extra virgin olive oil
- 4 butter (boston) lettuce leaves

PICKLED VEGETABLES

- 5 baby cucumbers (150g)
- 5 radishes (175g)
- 4 baby carrots (80g)
- ½ cup (125ml) white wine vinegar
- 2 tbsp caster (superfine) sugar

BEETROOT HUMMUS

- 1 medium beetroot (beet) (175g), grated coarsely
- 400g (12½oz) can chickpeas (garbanzo beans), drained, rinsed
- 1 clove garlic, crushed
- ¼ cup (60ml) lemon juice
- 1 tsp ground cumin

1 To make pickled vegetables, using a mandoline or knife, thinly slice cucumbers, radishes and carrots lengthways. Combine vegetables with vinegar and sugar in a glass or stainless steel bowl. Refrigerate for 30 minutes. Drain.

2 Meanwhile, to make beetroot hummus, process ingredients until smooth. Season. (Makes 2 cups.)

3 Process chickpeas, quinoa flakes, spices, green onion, chilli, coriander and the linseed meal until combined. Divide mixture into 8 portions; shape each portion into a 4cm x 6cm (1½in x 2½in) oval falafel.

4 Heat oil in a large non-stick frying pan over medium heat; cook falafels for 4 minutes, turning, until golden.

5 Spread beetroot hummus on the base of a shallow bowl, top with pickled vegetables and extra coriander. Serve with lettuce leaves and falafel.

PREP + COOK TIME 40 minutes **SERVES** 4

MISO & SEAWEED BREAD

- ¾ cup (150g) white quinoa
- ¼ cup (60ml) extra virgin olive oil
- ⅓ cup (80g) white (shiro) miso paste
- ¼ cup (60ml) maple syrup
- 2 cups (300g) wholemeal spelt flour
- ¼ cup (35g) arrowroot flour
- 2 tsp baking powder
- 2 tbsp pepitas (pumpkin seed kernels)
- 2 tbsp sesame seeds, plus 1 tbsp extra
- 2 tbsp dried wakame seaweed

1 Preheat oven to 180°C/350°F. Line a 10.5cm x 23.5cm (4in x 9½in) loaf pan with baking paper, extending the paper 3cm (1¼in) over the sides.

2 Place quinoa in a large heatproof bowl with enough hot water to cover; stand for 20 minutes. Drain; rinse well.

3 Whisk oil, miso and maple syrup in a large bowl until combined. Add soaked quinoa and 2½ cups (625ml) water; stir until combined. Sift flours and baking powder onto mixture, then add pepitas, sesame seeds and seaweed; stir until combined. Pour mixture into pan; sprinkle with extra sesame seeds. Cover with greased foil. Scrunch foil around sides of pan to secure.

4 Bake bread for 50 minutes or until firm to the touch. Increase oven to 200°C/400°F; bake, uncovered, for a further 25 minutes or until bread is golden and edges are crisp. Leave in pan for 5 minutes before transferring to a wire rack to cool completely.

5 Cut into slices for sandwiches or to toast.

PREP + COOK TIME 1½ hours (+ standing) **SERVES** 10

TIP Serve toasted slices topped with avocado, tomato and crumbled vegan fetta.

RICH IN
IODINE

WARM BARLEY, ASPARAGUS & PEA SALAD

- ¾ cup (150g) pearl barley
- 1 bunch asparagus (170g), cut into thirds on the diagonal
- ¾ cup (90g) frozen peas
- ¾ cup (190g) non-dairy yoghurt
- 2 tbsp lemon juice
- 1 tsp finely grated lemon rind
- 1 tbsp za'atar, plus extra to serve
- ½ tsp ground cumin
- 2 tbsp extra virgin olive oil
- 2 medium zucchini (240g), peeled into ribbons
- ¼ cup mint leaves, chopped finely
- ¼ cup dill, chopped coarsely
- 400g (12½oz) can chickpeas (garbanzo beans), drained, rinsed
- 1 long red chilli, sliced finely
- 250g (8oz) vegan fetta-style cheese, crumbled

1 Cook barley in a medium saucepan of boiling water for 35 minutes or until tender. Add asparagus and peas; cook for a further minute. Drain.

2 To make the dressing, whisk non-dairy yoghurt, lemon juice and rind, za'atar, cumin, olive oil and 2 tablespoons water in a small bowl until combined. Season to taste.

3 Place barley mixture in a medium bowl with zucchini, herbs, chickpeas, chilli and dressing; toss to combine, then season to taste. Serve topped with vegan fetta and extra za'atar.

PREP + COOK TIME 45 minutes **SERVES** 4

HASSELBACK EGGPLANT WITH MISO SOBA NOODLES

- 4 small eggplants (920g)
- 2 medium zucchini (240g), cut into 5mm (¼in) rounds
- 450g (14½oz) firm tofu, halved crossways, cut into 5mm (¼in) thick slices
- 1 clove garlic, crushed
- 1½ tbsp white (shiro) miso paste
- 2 tsp finely chopped fresh ginger
- 1½ tbsp reduced salt soy sauce
- 2 tsp sesame oil
- 2 tbsp extra virgin olive oil
- 4 green onions (scallions)
- 180g (5½oz) dried buckwheat soba noodles
- 1 tbsp sesame seeds, toasted
- ¼ cup (35g) roasted unsalted peanuts, chopped

1 Preheat oven to 180°C/350°F. Line a large oven tray with baking paper.

2 Cut a thin slice from base of each eggplant to sit flat. Cut through eggplants about 1cm (½in) apart, three quarters of the way through. Place eggplants on lined tray. Place slices of zucchini and tofu in the slits (the eggplant will fan out). Bake for 20 minutes.

3 Meanwhile, combine garlic, miso, ginger, soy sauce, sesame oil and olive oil in a small bowl.

4 Drizzle eggplants with half the miso mixture. Bake for a further 20 minutes or until eggplant is tender and lightly browned.

5 Meanwhile, cut green onions into long thin strips and place in chilled water to curl. Cook noodles according to packet directions; drain, then transfer to a large bowl and toss with remaining miso mixture.

6 Sprinkle hasselback eggplant with the sesame seeds, drained green onions and peanuts. Serve eggplant with noodles, drizzled with any cooking juices.

PREP + COOK TIME 50 minutes **SERVES** 4

GOOD
TO GO

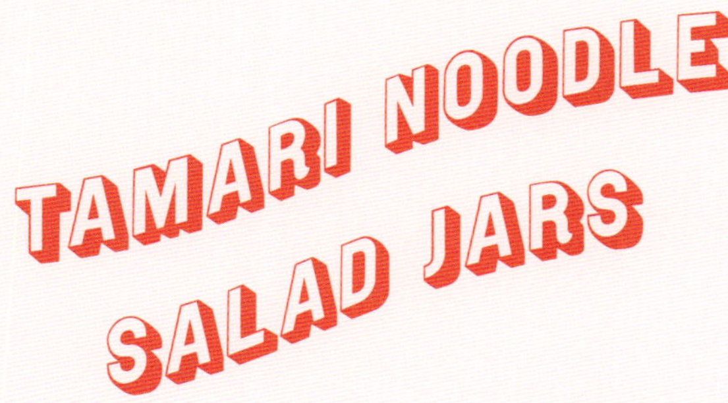

100g (3oz) dried soba noodles
2 small carrots (140g), grated coarsely
1 cup (80g) shredded red cabbage
250g (8oz) firm tofu, cubed
2 tbsp vegan kimchi (see tip)
1 cup (80g) bean sprouts
1 cup coriander (cilantro) leaves

GINGER SESAME DRESSING

6cm (2½in) piece fresh ginger
2 tbsp tamari
1 tbsp sesame oil
1 tbsp extra virgin olive oil
1 tbsp rice wine vinegar

1 Cook noodles in a medium saucepan of boiling water for 6 minutes or until tender. Drain; rinse under cold running water.

2 To make the ginger sesame dressing, peel and finely grate the ginger. Use your hands to squeeze the grated ginger over a small bowl to extract juice; you will need approximately 1 teaspoon of juice. Discard ginger pulp. Add remaining ingredients; stir to combine.

3 Divide noodles between two 3½-cup (875ml) jars with a lid; layer with carrot, cabbage, tofu, kimchi, bean sprouts and coriander. Cover jars with the lid. Refrigerate until required.

4 When ready to serve, pour contents into a bowl, then add dressing; toss gently to combine.

PREP + COOK TIME 20 minutes **SERVES** 2

TIP If you would like to make your own vegan kimchi see page 84.

EDAMAME, AVOCADO & SPINACH SOBA NOODLES

- 4 green tea bags
- 250g (8oz) buckwheat soba noodles
- 2 cups (300g) frozen shelled edamame (soybeans), thawed
- 1 tbsp sesame oil
- 2 green onions (scallions), sliced thinly
- 3 cloves garlic, sliced thinly
- 1 long green chilli, chopped finely
- 120g (4oz) baby spinach leaves
- 1 cup coriander (cilantro) leaves, chopped coarsely
- ¼ cup (60ml) lime juice
- 2 medium avocados (500g), chopped coarsely
- ½ cup (80g) almond kernels, roasted, chopped coarsely

1 Bring 3 litres (12 cups) water to the boil in a large saucepan. Turn off the heat. Add tea bags; steep for 10 minutes. Discard tea bags.

2 Fill a large bowl with cold water. Return tea water to the boil; add soba noodles, then cook for 5 minutes or until tender. Drain, reserving ½ cup (125ml) cooking liquid. Working quickly, refresh noodles in the cold water; drain. Cover until ready to serve.

3 Pat thawed edamame dry with paper towel. Heat oil in a wok or large frying pan over high heat. Add the green onion, garlic and chilli; cook, stirring frequently, for 1 minute or until fragrant. Add edamame; cook, stirring occasionally, for 2 minutes or until edamame are blistered slightly.

4 Add noodles to wok with spinach, half the coriander, the lime juice and reserved cooking liquid; cook, tossing continuously, for 2 minutes or until well combined and spinach has wilted.

5 Serve topped with avocado, remaining coriander and the almonds.

PREP + COOK TIME 30 minutes **SERVES** 4

TIPS Make sure you buy unsalted edamame as they are better for your health. Seed the chilli if you prefer less heat.

SWAP You can use peas instead of the edamame, if you like.

HIGH IN PROTEIN

SUPER
SPEEDY

OVEN-BAKED VEGIE SESAME TEMPURA

270g (8½oz) buckwheat soba noodles
1 tbsp sesame oil
½ cup (80g) sesame seeds, toasted, crushed
⅔ cup (120g) rice flour
2 tsp sea salt flakes
2½ tbsp vegan egg replacer
1 bunch broccolini (175g), trimmed, blanched (see tip)
150g (4½oz) oyster mushrooms
300g (9½oz) butternut pumpkin, unpeeled, sliced thinly
1 tbsp sesame seeds, extra, toasted

GINGER DRESSING

1½ tbsp tamari
⅓ cup (80ml) mirin
¼ cup (70g) pickled pink ginger, plus 2 tbsp pickling liquid
1 tsp sesame oil
1 baby cucumber (30g), chopped finely
1 green onion (scallion), sliced thinly

1 Cook soba noodles in a large saucepan of boiling water for 3 minutes or until just tender. Drain; refresh under cold running water until cool. Toss with sesame oil.
2 Preheat oven to 220°C/425°F. Line two large oven trays with baking paper.
3 Combine crushed sesame seeds, rice flour and salt flakes in a shallow bowl. Whisk egg replacer with 5 tbsp water until stiff in a second bowl.
4 Working in batches, dip broccolini, mushrooms and pumpkin into egg replacer mixture, then into the flour mixture, shaking to remove excess. Place on prepared trays. Bake, turning halfway, for 10 minutes or until crisp and golden.
5 Meanwhile, to make ginger dressing, place tamari, mirin, pickling liquid and sesame oil in a screw-top jar; shake well. Season to taste. Transfer to a small bowl; stir in cucumber, green onion and pickled ginger.
6 Arrange noodles on plates. Drizzle half the dressing over the noodles. Top with tempura vegies and serve with remaining dressing, sprinkled with extra sesame seeds.

PREP + COOK TIME 25 minutes **SERVES** 6

TIP To blanch broccolini, place in a heatproof bowl; pour over boiling water, stand until bright green. Drain, then place under cold running water until cooled. Pat dry with paper towel.

NOODLES

TANGY NOODLE SALAD WITH TOFU & PINEAPPLE

- 1 tbsp vegetable oil
- 500g (1lb) firm tofu, cut into 1cm (½in) cubes
- 3 cloves garlic, crushed
- ⅓ cup (100g) tamarind puree (see tip)
- 2 tbsp kecap manis
- 1 tbsp brown sugar
- ½ small pineapple (450g), cut into 2cm (¾in) pieces
- lime wedges, to serve

RICE NOODLE SALAD

- 100g (3oz) rice vermicelli
- 2 lebanese cucumbers (260g), julienned
- 240g (7½oz) cherry truss tomatoes, some halved
- ½ cup mint leaves
- ½ cup coriander (cilantro) leaves
- ½ cup thai basil leaves
- 2 tbsp lime juice
- 1 tbsp soy sauce
- 2 tsp olive oil

1 To make rice noodle salad, place noodles in a large heatproof bowl with enough boiling water to cover; stand for 2 minutes. Drain well. Return noodles to bowl with cucumber, tomato and herbs. Combine lime juice, soy sauce and oil in a small bowl. Add dressing to salad; toss gently to combine. Season to taste.

2 Heat a wok over high heat, then add oil; stir-fry tofu and garlic for 3 minutes on each side or until golden. Add combined tamarind, kecap manis, sugar and 1 tablespoon water, then pineapple; stir-fry until heated through.

3 Serve stir-fry with noodle salad and lime wedges.

PREP + COOK TIME 30 minutes **SERVES** 4

TIP Tamarind adds a tart, sweet and sour flavour to food. Tamarind puree is available in jars or plastic containers from major supermarkets and Asian grocers.

SUPER
SPEEDY

STEAMED, RICED, ROASTED

ALL IN THE FAMILY

CAULIFLOWER · BROCCOLI · GREEN VEGIES

The brassica (aka cabbage) family includes an array of versatile and diverse vegies from the flowering crowns of broccoli and cauliflower, to leafy asian greens and crisp salad vegies like radishes. Try them riced, steamed, roasted or munch on them raw to get your fix. No matter how you choose to eat them, these vegies offer fantastic flavour and potent health benefits.

ROASTED CAULIFLOWER & LENTIL SALAD

- 2 medium lemons (280g)
- ⅔ cup (160ml) extra virgin olive oil
- 2 cloves garlic, chopped
- 1 small cauliflower (680g), trimmed, cut into florets
- 400g (12½oz) can lentils, drained, rinsed
- 1 cup (200g) white quinoa
- 1 tbsp sherry vinegar
- ½ cup flat-leaf parsley leaves
- ½ cup small mint leaves
- 2 green onions (scallions), sliced thinly
- 100g (3oz) vegan fetta-style cheese, crumbled
- ¼ cup (50g) pomegranate seeds

1 Preheat oven to 200°C/400°F. Line two oven trays with baking paper.

2 Finely grate rind from lemons. Squeeze juice from lemons; you will need ¼ cup (60ml) juice. Combine ⅓ cup (80ml) oil, garlic and lemon rind in a small bowl.

3 Place cauliflower on one lined tray; drizzle with half the oil mixture, then season. Toss to coat. Roast cauliflower for 30 minutes or until golden and tender.

4 Meanwhile, pat the lentils dry with paper towel. Place in a single layer on second lined tray; drizzle with remaining oil mixture, then season. Stir to coat. Roast lentils for 20 minutes, stirring occasionally, until crisp. Cool on tray.

5 Rinse quinoa in a sieve under cold running water. Place quinoa and 2 cups (500ml) water in a medium saucepan; bring to the boil. Reduce heat to low; cook, covered, for 15 minutes or until quinoa is tender. Drain; cool.

6 Combine vinegar, lemon juice and remaining oil in a large bowl; season. Add parsley, mint, green onion, cauliflower and quinoa, season to taste; toss gently to combine. Serve topped with crisp lentils, crumbled vegan fetta and pomegranate seeds.

PREP + COOK TIME 40 minutes (+ cooling) **SERVES** 4

GOOD
TO GO

SPICED CAULIFLOWER SOUP WITH CHICKPEA CROÛTONS

CAULI-FLOWER

- 3 tsp extra virgin olive oil
- 1 tbsp vegan madras curry paste
- 1 medium onion (150g), sliced thinly
- 2 cloves garlic, crushed
- 1½ tsp cumin seeds
- 1 tsp coriander seeds
- 750g (1½lb) cauliflower florets
- 2 medium tomatoes (300g), peeled, seeded, chopped finely
- 2½ cups (625ml) vegetable stock
- 400g (12½oz) can chickpeas (garbanzo beans), drained, rinsed
- ⅓ cup (80ml) canned light coconut milk
- ¼ cup coriander (cilantro) leaves
- 1 long red chilli, sliced thinly
- lime wedges, to serve

CHICKPEA CROÛTONS

- 400g (12½oz) can chickpeas (garbanzo beans), drained, rinsed
- 1 tsp extra virgin olive oil
- ½ tsp ground cumin

1 Heat oil in a large heavy-based saucepan over medium heat. Add curry paste, onion, garlic, cumin seeds, coriander seeds and cauliflower. Cook, stirring, for 5 minutes or until cauliflower starts to soften. Add tomato, stock and 1½ cups (375ml) water; bring to the boil. Reduce heat to low; cook, covered, for 20 minutes or until vegetables are very soft. Add chickpeas; cook for 2 minutes or until warmed through.

2 Meanwhile, preheat oven to 220°C/425°F.

3 To make chickpea croûtons, grease and line a small oven tray with baking paper. Toss chickpeas with oil and cumin to coat; spread over tray. Bake for 15 minutes or until chickpeas are crisp and golden.

4 Cool cauliflower mixture slightly; blend or process until smooth. Return to pan, add coconut milk; stir over low heat until heated through.

5 Divide soup among bowls; top with chickpea croûtons, coriander leaves and chilli. Season with pepper and serve with lime wedges.

PREP + COOK TIME 40 minutes **SERVES** 4

CAULIFLOWER, GINGER & TOFU CURRY

CAULI-FLOWER

- 2 x 4cm pieces fresh ginger (40g)
- ¼ cup (60ml) extra virgin olive oil
- 8 shallots, halved
- 2 tbsp curry powder
- 1 tsp ground turmeric
- 400ml can light coconut cream
- 1 cup (250ml) vegetable stock
- ½ large cauliflower (1kg), cut into large florets
- 450g (14½oz) firm tofu, cut into 2.5cm (1in) pieces
- 1¼ cups (150g) frozen peas
- ⅓ cup curry leaves
- 2 cloves garlic, sliced thinly
- steamed brown rice and lime wedges, to serve

1 Peel ginger pieces; finely grate one piece and thinly slice the remaining piece. Keep separate.
2 Heat 1 tablespoon oil in a large, heavy-based saucepan over medium heat. Cook shallots, covered, for 2 minutes or until starting to soften and edges are turning golden.
3 Add curry powder, turmeric and the grated ginger; cook, stirring, for 30 seconds. Add coconut cream and stock; cook, scraping the base of the pan with a wooden spoon, until well combined. Add cauliflower and tofu; cook, covered, stirring halfway though, for 15 minutes or until cauliflower is just tender. Add the peas for the last 2 minutes of cooking time. Season.
4 Meanwhile, heat remaining oil in a small, heavy-based saucepan over medium heat. Taking care as the oil will splutter, add sliced ginger, curry leaves and garlic. Cook, stirring frequently, for 2 minutes or until crisp. Stir half the ginger mixture through curry.
5 Top curry with remaining ginger mixture. Serve with steamed brown rice and lime wedges.

PREP + COOK TIME 35 minutes **SERVES** 4

SMOKY BAKED WHOLE CAULIFLOWER

- 1.3kg (2¾lb) whole cauliflower
- 1 cup (250ml) vegetable stock
- 60g (2oz) vegan spread, melted (see tip)
- 1 tsp smoked paprika
- 1 clove garlic, crushed
- ¼ cup (20g) grated vegan parmesan-style cheese
- 2 tbsp chopped flat-leaf parsley

1 Preheat oven to 200°C/400°F.
2 Cut a cross into the base of the cauliflower with a sharp knife. Place in a large, heavy-based casserole dish or roasting pan. Pour stock into dish.
3 Combine melted vegan spread, smoked paprika, garlic and vegan parmesan in a small bowl; season. Brush over cauliflower. Cover dish with a lid or foil.
4 Bake for 20 minutes. Remove lid; bake, uncovered, for a further 15 minutes or until cauliflower is tender and browned. Sprinkle with parsley. Season.

PREP + COOK TIME 45 minutes **SERVES** 4 (or 6 as a side)

TIP You can use a 'butter-flavoured' plant spread or extra virgin olive oil.

CAULIFLOWER GNOCCHI WITH SILVERBEET

1kg (2lb) cauliflower, cut into 3cm (1¼in) florets (see tip)

1½ cups (225g) white spelt flour, plus extra to dust

¼ tsp ground nutmeg

⅓ cup (80ml) extra virgin olive oil

1 bunch silverbeet (swiss chard) (750g), stems sliced very thinly, leaves torn

2 tsp finely grated lemon rind

2 tbsp lemon juice

⅓ cup (45g) coarsely chopped roasted hazelnuts

½ tsp chilli flakes

PREP + COOK TIME 50 minutes
SERVES 4

TIP After you have trimmed the cauliflower, weigh it, as you will need 850g (1¾lb) to make the gnocchi.

1 Steam cauliflower in a covered steamer basket, over a saucepan of boiling water, for 8 minutes or until tender. Transfer cauliflower to a clean tea towel, cool for 5 minutes. Squeeze out as much excess liquid as possible, until cauliflower feels dry.
2 Process cauliflower with flour, nutmeg, salt and pepper until mixture just comes together as a ball of dough. Turn dough out onto a lightly floured surface; knead gently until smooth. Cut dough into 4 equal portions; cover with a clean tea towel.
3 Roll each dough portion into a 2cm (¾in) thick rope, about 29cm (11¾in) long. Cut into 2cm (¾in) pieces. Transfer to a lightly floured tray.
4 Cook gnocchi in a large saucepan of boiling salted water, in batches, for 3 minutes or until gnocchi float to the surface. Remove gnocchi from pan with a slotted spoon. Transfer to an oiled tray; reserve ½ cup (125ml) cooking water.
5 Heat 2 tablespoons oil in a large, deep frying pan over medium heat. Cook gnocchi, tossing, for 3 minutes or until golden brown. Remove from pan. Heat remaining oil in the same pan over medium heat; cook silverbeet stems for 3 minutes or until almost soft. Add silverbeet leaves and the reserved cooking water; cook, stirring, for 1 minute or until just wilted. Stir in lemon rind and juice; season well. Remove pan from heat.
6 Divide silverbeet mixture among bowls; top with gnocchi, and scatter over hazelnuts and chilli flakes.

GOOD TO GO

CAULIFLOWER FILLO TRIANGLES

- 2 tbsp olive oil
- 2 medium red onions (340g), chopped finely
- 2 cloves garlic, crushed
- 1 tsp ground turmeric
- 1 tsp ground ginger
- ¾ tsp ground cinnamon
- ½ medium cauliflower (750g), chopped finely
- 1 cup (160g) roasted blanched almonds, chopped coarsely
- 1 cup coarsely chopped coriander (cilantro)
- 1 cup coarsely chopped flat-leaf parsley
- 10 sheets fillo pastry
- ½ cup (125ml) olive oil, extra
- lemon wedges, to serve

1 Heat oil in a large frying pan over medium-high heat; cook the onion, garlic, turmeric, ginger and ½ teaspoon ground cinnamon for 5 minutes or until onion softens. Add cauliflower; cook, stirring, for 10 minutes or until tender. Season with salt; transfer mixture to a large bowl. Stir in almonds and herbs. Cool completely.

2 Preheat oven to 180°C/350°F. Oil an oven tray.

3 Brush 1 sheet of pastry with a little of the extra oil; cut in half lengthways, place one strip on the other. Place ⅓ cup cauliflower mixture in a corner of pastry strip, leaving a 1cm (½in) border. Fold opposite corner of pastry diagonally across filling to form a triangle; continue folding to the end of pastry strip, retaining triangular shape. Place triangle, seam-side down, on tray. Repeat with remaining pastry sheets, a little more oil and the cauliflower filling to make 10 triangles in total.

4 Brush cauliflower triangles with a little more oil; dust with the remaining cinnamon. Bake for 50 minutes or until golden. Serve with lemon wedges.

PREP + COOK TIME 1 hour 20 minutes (+ cooling)
MAKES 10

CREAMY BROCCOLI SOUP WITH CRUNCHY QUINOA

- 1 tbsp olive oil
- 1 medium leek (350g), sliced thinly
- 2 stalks celery (300g), trimmed, chopped finely
- 2 cloves garlic, crushed
- 1 large head broccoli (400g), cut into florets
- 2 medium zucchini (240g), chopped coarsely
- 1 large potato (300g), peeled, chopped coarsely
- 2¼ cups (560ml) vegetable stock
- ⅓ cup (95g) non-dairy yoghurt
- soy and linseed bread, toasted, to serve

CRUNCHY QUINOA

- ½ cup (100g) white quinoa, rinsed well
- 2 tbsp olive oil
- 2 tbsp sunflower seeds
- 2 tbsp chopped roasted almonds
- 1 tsp chilli flakes
- 2 cloves garlic, crushed
- 2 tbsp chopped flat-leaf parsley

1 Heat oil in a large heavy-based saucepan over medium-high heat. Add leek and celery; cook, stirring, for 3 minutes or until softened. Add garlic; cook for 1 minute or until fragrant.

2 Add broccoli, zucchini, potato, vegetable stock and 2¾ cups (680ml) water to pan; bring to the boil. Reduce heat to low-medium; simmer for 10 minutes or until vegetables are tender. Remove soup from heat; cool slightly.

3 Meanwhile, to make crunchy quinoa, cook quinoa according to packet directions; drain well. Heat oil in a medium frying pan over medium heat. Add quinoa, sunflower seeds, almonds and chilli flakes; cook, stirring, for 10 minutes or until quinoa browns lightly. Add garlic and parsley; cook, stirring, for 1 minute or until fragrant. Transfer to a plate to cool. (Quinoa will crisp as it cools.)

4 Blend or process soup until smooth. Return soup to pan over medium heat; stir until hot.

5 Divide soup among bowls; top with non-dairy yoghurt and season to taste. Sprinkle with crunchy quinoa and serve with toast.

PREP + COOK TIME 40 minutes **SERVES** 4

SUPER SPEEDY

ROASTED BROCCOLINI, EDAMAME & CHILLI TEMPEH SALAD

300g (9½oz) chickpea tempeh
2 long red chillies
1 tbsp tamari
1 tbsp maple syrup
2 bunches broccolini (350g)
2 cups (300g) frozen shelled edamame (soybeans)
2 tbsp peanut oil
60g (2oz) mixed salad leaves
lime halves, to serve

CASHEW DRESSING

2 tbsp cashew spread
1½ tbsp lime juice
1 tbsp tamari
1 tbsp peanut oil

1 Heat oven to 200°C/400°F. Line two large oven trays with baking paper.

2 Using your hands, gently crumble tempeh into a bowl, forming a mixture of large and small chunks. Finely chop 1 chilli; add to bowl with tamari and maple syrup. Toss gently to combine. Spread mixture over one tray.

3 Place the broccolini and edamame on remaining tray; drizzle with oil, then toss to combine. Season. Roast the tempeh and vegetables for 15 minutes or until broccolini is just tender and tempeh is golden.

4 Meanwhile, to make cashew dressing, whisk the ingredients together with 1 tablespoon cold water in a small bowl until smooth. Add an extra tablespoon of cold water if necessary to thin. (Makes ½ cup.)

5 Combine broccolini, edamame and salad leaves in a large bowl. Divide among plates; top with tempeh and drizzle with the dressing. Scatter with remaining sliced chilli; serve with lime halves.

PREP + COOK TIME 25 minutes **SERVES** 4

BROCCOLI & TOFU SAAC CURRY

400g (12½oz) firm tofu, cut into 2cm (¾in) pieces
2 tsp curry powder
2 tbsp extra virgin olive oil
2 large heads broccoli (800g), cut into florets
1 medium onion (150g), chopped finely
1 bunch coriander (cilantro), leaves reserved, stems and roots chopped finely
2 tbsp grated fresh ginger
2 tsp garam masala
400g (12½oz) can diced tomatoes
2½ cups (625ml) vegetable stock
1 bunch english spinach (300g), washed, leaves picked
300g (9½oz) sugar snap peas, trimmed
2 tbsp lemon juice

1 Pat tofu dry with paper towel then toss with curry powder. Heat 1 tablespoon oil in a large, deep frying pan over high heat. Cook the tofu, turning, for 3 minutes or until golden on all sides. Transfer to a large bowl. Cook three-quarters of the broccoli in same pan for 3 minutes or until browned; add to bowl with tofu.

2 Reduce heat to medium. Heat remaining oil in same pan; cook onion, ½ cup coriander roots and stems, the ginger and garam masala, stirring, for 5 minutes or until softened. Add the tomato and stock; bring to the boil. Cook for 8 minutes or until reduced slightly.

3 Process remaining broccoli and the spinach leaves until finely chopped. Stir into curry.

4 Return the tofu and cooked broccoli to pan with the sugar snap peas; cook for 3 minutes or until warmed through. Stir through lemon juice.

5 Serve curry topped with reserved coriander leaves.

PREP + COOK TIME 40 minutes **SERVES** 4

SERVING Serve curry with crisp flatbreads or brown rice.

BROCCOLI 'MEATBALL' GREEN CURRY

- 2 small carrots (140g)
- 1 small zucchini (90g)
- 100g (3oz) broccoli florets, chopped finely
- 3 cloves garlic, crushed
- 2 tsp finely grated ginger
- ⅓ cup coriander (cilantro) leaves, chopped finely, plus extra leaves to serve
- 1 tbsp pine nuts, toasted
- 2 tbsp linseed (flaxseed) meal
- 1½ cups (180g) almond meal
- 1 cup (70g) fine dry breadcrumbs
- ⅓ cup (80ml) extra virgin olive oil
- 2 x 270ml cans coconut cream
- 2 tbsp vegan thai green curry paste
- 400g (12½oz) cauliflower, florets chopped coarsely, stems discarded
- 2 tsp ground turmeric
- 1 long green chilli, chopped finely

1 Finely grate carrots into a bowl. Finely grate zucchini onto a piece of baking paper; using hands, squeeze out excess moisture, then add to bowl with carrot. Add the broccoli, garlic, ginger, chopped coriander and pine nuts; combine well. Add linseed meal and almond meal; mix well.

2 Place breadcrumbs in a small bowl. Using damp hands, form heaped tablespoons of vegetable mixture into balls to make 24 in total. Roll in breadcrumbs to coat.

3 Heat ¼ cup (60ml) olive oil in a large, non-stick frying pan over medium heat; fry 'meatballs', in two batches, turning occasionally, for 4 minutes. Remove 'meatballs' from pan; wipe pan clean with paper towel.

4 Stir coconut cream and curry paste in cleaned pan; increase heat to high. Simmer for 5 minutes or until thickened and reduced. Return 'meatballs' to pan; turn gently to coat in sauce.

5 Place cauliflower in a food processor; pulse until it resembles rice. Heat remaining 1 tablespoon of olive oil in a medium frying pan over high heat; cook cauliflower and turmeric, stirring frequently, for 4 minutes or until just tender.

6 Serve 'meatball' curry with cauliflower rice, topped with chilli and extra coriander. Season with pepper.

PREP + COOK TIME 35 minutes **SERVES** 4

SUPER SPROUT SPAGHETTI BOLOGNESE

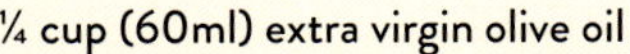

- ¼ cup (60ml) extra virgin olive oil
- 500g (1lb) brussels sprouts, trimmed
- 1 large onion (200g), chopped finely
- 1 small carrot (70g), grated coarsely
- 4 cloves garlic, crushed
- 1 tbsp finely chopped rosemary
- ⅓ cup (95g) tomato paste
- 2 x 400g (12½oz) cans diced tomatoes with italian herbs
- 2 x 250g (8oz) packets dried pulse spaghetti (see tip)
- ⅓ cup basil leaves
- finely grated vegan parmesan-style cheese, to serve

1 Heat 1½ tablespoons of the oil in a large saucepan over high heat; cook brussels sprouts, stirring occasionally, for 10 minutes or until browned. Remove from pan.

2 Heat the remaining oil in same pan over medium heat; cook onion and carrot, stirring, for 3 minutes or until softened. Add garlic, rosemary and tomato paste; cook, stirring, for 2 minutes or until paste darkens slightly. Add canned tomatoes and ¾ cup (180ml) water; bring to the boil. Reduce heat to low; simmer, covered, for 10 minutes.

3 Meanwhile, cook pasta in a large saucepan of boiling salted water following packet directions until tender; drain. Return pasta to pan.

4 Add sprouts and half the basil to sauce; cook, stirring, for 2 minutes or until heated through. Season to taste.

5 Serve pasta topped with bolognese, remaining basil and the vegan parmesan.

PREP + COOK TIME 40 minutes **SERVES** 4

TIP We used pulse spaghetti made from peas, lentils, chickpeas (garbanzo beans) and borlotti beans.

HIGH IN
FIBRE

CABBAGE & CARROT FILLO PIE WITH SEED TOPPING

- ½ cup (125ml) extra virgin olive oil
- 1 large leek (500g), white part only, sliced thinly
- 3 cloves garlic, crushed
- 2 tsp caraway seeds
- 3 medium carrots (360g), grated coarsely
- 375g (12oz) savoy cabbage, shredded
- ⅓ cup (55g) currants
- ⅓ cup finely chopped mint
- 14 sheets fillo pastry
- non-dairy yoghurt, to serve

SEED TOPPING

- ¼ cup (50g) pepitas (pumpkin seed kernels)
- ¼ cup (35g) slivered almonds
- ¼ cup (25g) coarsely chopped walnuts
- 1 tbsp poppy seeds
- 1 tbsp sesame seeds

1 Heat ¼ cup of the oil in a large frying pan over medium heat; cook leek, garlic and caraway seeds, stirring, for 5 minutes. Add carrot; cook for 3 minutes. Add cabbage; cook for a further 5 minutes or until vegetables are soft. Stir in currants and mint. Cool.
2 To make seed topping, combine ingredients in a small bowl.
3 Preheat oven to 180°C/350°F. Oil a 25cm (10in) springform pan.
4 Divide filling into seven portions. Brush one sheet of pastry with a little of the remaining oil; top with a second sheet. Place one portion of filling lengthways, in a thin line, along pastry edge; roll pastry to enclose filling. Starting at the centre of springform pan, carefully form the pastry roll, seam-side down, into a coil. Repeat with remaining pastry sheets, a little more oil and the filling portions, joining each roll to the end of the last one and coiling it around until the base of the pan is covered. Brush top with remaining oil.
5 Bake fillo pie for 20 minutes. Cover pie evenly with seed topping; bake for a further 10 minutes or until golden. Serve with non-dairy yoghurt.

PREP + COOK TIME 1 hour (+ cooling) **SERVES** 6

TIP After unwrapping fillo in step 4, cover any sheets you aren't using immediately with baking paper, then a damp tea towel to prevent drying out.

EASY VEGAN KIMCHI

You need to sterilise a 1-litre (4-cup) glass jar and lid before you start. For information on how to sterilise jars, see glossary page 160.

500g (1lb) savoy cabbage
½ small daikon (200g), peeled, julienned
1 medium carrot (120g), julienned
2 green onions (scallions), sliced thinly
1 tbsp sea salt flakes
3 cups (750ml) filtered water
2 tbsp gochujang (see tips)
2 tsp finely grated ginger
1 clove garlic, crushed

VEGAN 'FISH' SAUCE

1 sheet toasted nori, torn
2 tbsp lime juice
1½ tbsp tamari
2 tsp red (aka) miso paste

1 Remove outer leaf from cabbage; reserve. Cut the cabbage into 2.5cm (1in) pieces. Place cabbage, daikon, carrot and green onion in a large bowl. Rub the salt into vegetables until cabbage softens. Add the filtered water. Place a plate or bowl directly on vegetables, weighted down with food cans; stand for 1 hour.

2 Meanwhile, to make the vegan 'fish' sauce, blend or process ingredients until as smooth as possible. Store in a jar in the fridge until required. (Makes ⅓ cup.)

3 Combine gochujang, ginger, garlic and 1 tablespoon of the vegan 'fish' sauce in a small bowl.

4 Drain cabbage mixture, then rinse; squeeze out the excess liquid. Combine cabbage and gochujang mixtures. Transfer to a 1-litre (4-cup) sterilised glass jar. Press down firmly on the mixture, leaving a 1cm (½in) space at top of the jar to allow for fermentation.

5 Place reserved cabbage leaf directly on cabbage mixture in jar. Press down firmly to cover; seal jar.

6 Store jar at room temperature, away from direct sunlight, for 1-3 days or until fermented (see tips). Refrigerate for up to 1 month.

PREP TIME 30 minutes (+ standing & 1-3 days fermenting)
MAKES 4 cups

TIPS Gochujang is a Korean fermented chilli paste with a smoky spicy-sweet flavour; it is available from Asian grocers. Substitute with a paste made from 3 long red chillies and a pinch of smoked paprika. Depending on the ambient room temperature fermentation will vary from 1-3 days or even longer. Check the taste of the kimchi daily; it should taste pleasantly sour with a hint of sweetness. Refrigerate kimchi once fermented.

GREENS & TOMATO WHOLEMEAL GALETTE

- ¼ cup (60ml) extra virgin olive oil
- 2 cloves garlic, crushed
- 400g (12½oz) can butter beans, drained, rinsed
- 4 cups (140g) loosely packed shredded curly kale
- ½ bunch silverbeet (swiss chard) (375g), chopped
- 1 tsp chilli flakes
- 500g (1lb) cocktail truss tomatoes
- ¼ cup (40g) pine nuts
- 6 thyme sprigs

PASTRY

- 1 tbsp chia seeds
- ⅔ cup (160ml) soda water
- 2 cups (300g) wholemeal spelt flour
- 1 cup (150g) white spelt flour
- ¾ cup (180ml) extra virgin olive oil
- 2 tbsp thyme leaves
- 1 tsp sea salt flakes

1 Preheat oven to 220°C/425°F.

2 To make pastry, stir chia seeds and 2 tablespoons of the soda water in a small bowl; stand for 3 minutes. Process the flours, oil, thyme, salt, chia mixture and remaining soda water until mixture just forms a dough. Transfer to a clean work surface; shape into a disc. Wrap in plastic wrap; refrigerate until needed.

3 Heat 2 tablespoons of the oil in a large non-stick frying pan over medium heat. Cook garlic, stirring, for 30 seconds. Add beans, kale, silverbeet, chilli flakes and ¼ cup (60ml) water, season; cook for 5 minutes or until greens have wilted and liquid is evaporated. Cool.

4 Roll pastry out between two sheets of baking paper into a 35cm x 45cm (14in x 17in) oval. Remove top layer of paper. Lift pastry on paper to a large oven tray. Spoon greens mixture into the centre of the pastry, leaving a 4cm (1½in) border around the edge. Using paper as an aide, fold in the pastry border, pleating it slightly as you go to form a pastry crust.

5 Bake galette on bottom shelf of oven for 20 minutes. Place tomatoes, pine nuts and thyme sprigs on galette; drizzle with remaining oil. Reduce oven to 180°C/350°F; bake galette for a further 15 minutes or until pastry is golden and cooked through. Serve galette warm.

PREP + COOK TIME 1 hour 5 minutes (+ cooling)
SERVES 4

GAI LAN & MUSHROOM NOODLE STIR-FRY

- 450g (14½oz) thin udon-style noodles
- 2 tbsp peanut oil
- 2 cloves garlic, crushed
- 1 long red chilli, sliced thinly
- ½ tsp chinese five-spice powder
- 430g (14oz) gai lan
- 2 tbsp vegetarian oyster sauce (see tip)
- 2 tbsp kecap manis
- ½ tsp sesame oil
- 200g (6½oz) enoki mushrooms, trimmed
- 2 tbsp fried shallots

1 Place the noodles in a medium heatproof bowl with enough boiling water to cover; separate the noodles with a fork. Drain.

2 Heat peanut oil in a wok over high heat; stir-fry garlic and chilli for 1 minute or until softened. Add five-spice and gai lan; stir-fry for 1 minute or until tender.

3 Add sauces, sesame oil and drained noodles; stir-fry for 1 minute or until noodles are heated through. Toss through mushrooms.

4 Serve stir-fry topped with shallots.

PREP + COOK TIME 20 minutes **SERVES** 4

TIP While regular oyster sauce is made from oysters and their brine, vegetarian oyster sauce is made from mushrooms.

SUPER
SPEEDY

GOOD
TO GO

ZUCCHINI KOFTAS WITH SMOKY TOMATO AÏOLI

- 250g (8oz) potatoes, scrubbed, halved
- 500g (1lb) zucchini, grated coarsely
- 1 long green chilli, chopped finely
- 4 green onions (scallions), chopped finely
- ½ cup (90g) rice flour
- sunflower oil, for shallow-frying
- soft-leafed herbs of your choice, to serve

SMOKY TOMATO AÏOLI

- 2 tbsp chopped sun-dried tomatoes
- 1 chipotle chilli in adobo sauce
- 1 clove garlic, chopped
- ½ cup (150g) vegan mayonnaise

1 Place potatoes in a small saucepan; cover with water. Bring to the boil; cook for 25 minutes or until tender. Drain, return to pan and coarsely mash with a fork.

2 Meanwhile, to make smoky tomato aïoli, place sun-dried tomatoes in a small bowl; cover with boiling water. Stand for 15 minutes; drain. Stir through remaining ingredients until combined (or blend until smooth); season to taste.

3 Place grated zucchini in a clean tea towel; squeeze over sink to remove excess moisture. Place zucchini in a large bowl; add mashed potato, chilli, green onion and rice flour. Season; mix well to combine.

4 Heat 2cm (¾in) oil in a large frying pan over high heat. Shape ¼-cup measures of the zucchini mixture into ovals to make 12 in total. Shallow-fry koftas, in batches, for 3 minutes each side or until golden and crisp. Remove with a slotted spoon; drain on paper towel.

5 Scatter koftas with herbs and serve with aïoli.

PREP + COOK TIME 45 minutes **SERVES** 4

SILVERBEET & VEGAN HALOUMI PIE

- ¼ cup (60ml) extra virgin olive oil
- 350g (11oz) swiss brown mushrooms, halved
- 2 tbsp lemon thyme leaves, chopped finely
- 4 cloves garlic, crushed
- 1 cup (180g) pitted green sicilian olives
- 400g (12½oz) can diced tomatoes
- 500g (1lb) silverbeet (swiss chard), trimmed, chopped coarsely
- ⅓ cup (50g) pine nuts, toasted
- 150g (4½oz) vegan haloumi-style cheese, grated coarsely
- 6 sheets fillo pastry
- ¼ cup (50g) couscous
- 8 lemon thyme sprigs

PREP + COOK TIME
45 minutes (+ cooling)
SERVES 4

TIP After unwrapping the fillo in step 6, cover any sheets you aren't using immediately with baking paper, then a damp tea towel to prevent drying out.

1 Preheat oven to 220°C/425°F.
2 Heat 2 teaspoons of the oil in a 22cm (8¾in) (base measurement) deep, ovenproof frying pan over high heat. Cook the mushrooms, chopped thyme and garlic, stirring occasionally, for 5 minutes or until mushrooms are golden.
3 Coarsely chop three-quarters of the olives; leave the remaining olives whole.
4 Add tomato and chopped olives to pan with mushrooms; cook for 5 minutes or until thickened. Add silverbeet; cook, stirring, for 1 minute or until wilted. Transfer to a large bowl; season to taste. Cool. Wipe pan clean and reserve.
5 Finely chop ¼ cup pine nuts; combine with vegan haloumi in a small bowl.
6 Lightly brush reserved pan with some of the remaining oil. Lightly brush one sheet of fillo with oil and sprinkle with 2 tablespoons of the vegan haloumi mixture. Top with a second sheet of fillo. Repeat with oil, haloumi mixture and fillo to create a stack of three sheets. Place in the frying pan, with edges overhanging. Repeat with remaining fillo, a little more oil and the haloumi mixture to create a second stack; place crossways in frying pan. Sprinkle top with remaining haloumi mixture and the uncooked couscous.
7 Squeeze excess liquid from mushroom mixture. Spoon the cooled mushroom mixture into the pan. Fold over the fillo to cover most of the pie leaving a 6cm (2½in) uncovered round in the centre for steam to escape. Brush pastry top with remaining oil. Place pan on an oven tray.
8 Bake pie for 18 minutes; top with thyme sprigs and bake for a further 2 minutes or until golden. Top with remaining olives and pine nuts.

VITAL FOODS FOR VEGANS

MEET YOUR PROTEIN

TOFU • NUTS & SEEDS • PLANT-BASED MINCE

Quality sources of minimally processed vegan protein are to be found in soy-based tofu and tempeh, which can be sautéed, stir-fried, scrambled, coated or formed into patties for recipes that mirror meat and egg dishes. Not to be forgotten are legumes, seeds and nutrient dense nuts. There are also numerous widely available mock meat alternatives like plant-based minces. These offer processed-food convenience but should be used more sparingly along with wholefood options for a balanced vegan diet.

MEXICAN LIME TOFU WRAPS WITH SLAW

- 1 bunch coriander (cilantro)
- ⅓ cup (80ml) lime juice
- 2 long red chillies, seeded, chopped finely
- ¼ cup (60ml) extra virgin olive oil
- 300g (9½oz) firm tofu, cut into 8 long slices
- 1 large avocado (320g)
- ½ clove garlic, crushed
- 1 medium carrot (120g), julienned
- 1 medium purple carrot (120g), julienned
- 2 cups (160g) shredded savoy cabbage
- 4 radishes (140g), trimmed, sliced thinly
- 8 wholegrain tortillas, warmed
- lime wedges, to serve

1 Wash coriander well to remove all dirt from stems. Pick leaves from coriander; reserve for slaw. Finely chop roots and stems.

2 Combine coriander root and stem mix, 2 tablespoons lime juice, half the chilli and 1 tablespoon oil in a shallow bowl. Add tofu; toss to coat well. Cover; refrigerate for at least 2 hours or overnight.

3 To make guacamole, coarsely mash avocado in a bowl; stir in garlic, 1 tablespoon lime juice and the remaining chilli. Season to taste.

4 To make dressing, combine 1 tablespoon oil and the remaining lime juice in a small jug; season to taste.

5 Place carrots, cabbage, radish and reserved coriander leaves in a large bowl with the dressing; toss to combine.

6 Drain tofu well; reserve marinade. Heat remaining oil in a medium frying pan over medium-high heat. Cook tofu for 1 minute each side or until golden.

7 Serve tortillas topped with slaw, guacamole and tofu; drizzle with reserved marinade. Serve with lime wedges.

PREP + COOK TIME 35 minutes (+ refrigeration)
SERVES 4

SWAP Swap purple carrot for an extra orange carrot or use ½ small red capsicum (bell pepper) instead.

GOOD
TO GO

SUSHI SALAD BOWL WITH SOY GLAZED TOFU

- ½ cup (125ml) soy sauce
- ⅓ cup (75g) caster (superfine) sugar
- 1½ tbsp finely grated fresh ginger
- ⅓ cup (80ml) rice wine vinegar
- 1 tbsp sesame oil
- 600g (1¼lb) medium tofu, cut into 1cm (½in) slices
- 2 tbsp teriyaki sauce
- 450g (14½oz) packet microwave brown rice
- 1 large carrot (180g), julienned
- 4 baby cucumbers (130g), chopped
- 2 small avocados (400g), cut into wedges
- ¼ cup (70g) pickled ginger
- 1 tbsp sesame seeds, toasted

1 Preheat oven to 220°C/425°F. Line an oven tray with baking paper.

2 Place soy sauce, sugar, 1 tablespoon of the grated ginger, 2 tablespoons of the vinegar and the oil in a small saucepan; cook, stirring, over high heat for 4 minutes or until thickened. Reserve half the marinade in a small jug.

3 Place tofu slices on lined tray; brush both sides with remaining marinade. Roast tofu for 8 minutes or until golden and almost heated through.

4 Meanwhile, combine teriyaki sauce and the remaining grated ginger and vinegar in a medium bowl. Heat rice following packet directions. Combine warm rice and teriyaki dressing in bowl.

5 Divide rice mixture evenly among serving bowls; top with carrot, tofu, cucumber, avocado and pickled ginger; drizzle with reserved marinade. Serve sprinkled with sesame seeds.

PREP + COOK TIME 45 minutes **SERVES** 4

JAPANESE-STYLE TOFU SALAD

- 500g (1lb) silken firm tofu
- 500g (1lb) microwave brown and wild rice
- 1 cup (150g) frozen shelled edamame (soybeans)
- 50g (1½oz) snow pea tendrils or shoots
- 1 bunch asparagus (170g), trimmed, sliced thinly lengthways
- 4 green onions (scallions), sliced thinly
- ¼ cup (70g) pickled pink ginger, shredded
- ½ cup (90g) brown rice flour
- sunflower oil, for shallow-frying
- 2 sheets nori (5g), shredded finely
- 1 tbsp sesame seeds, toasted

SOY DRESSING

- ¼ cup (60ml) light soy sauce
- 2 tbsp mirin
- 1 tbsp extra virgin olive oil
- 1 tbsp lime juice

1 Drain tofu and gently press between sheets of paper towel to remove as much moisture as possible.
2 To make soy dressing, place ingredients in a screw-top jar; shake well to combine.
3 Reheat rice according to packet directions. Place the edamame in a large heatproof bowl, cover with boiling water; stand until thawed. Drain; refresh under cold running water, then return to bowl. Add rice, snow pea tendrils, asparagus, green onion, ginger and soy dressing; toss well to combine.
4 Cut tofu into 3cm (1¼in) pieces. Place in a large bowl with rice flour; season with salt and white pepper. Gently turn to coat, taking care not to break up the tofu.
5 Heat 2cm (¾in) oil in a deep frying pan over medium heat; cook tofu for 2 minutes each side or until golden. Remove with a slotted spoon, drain on paper towel.
6 Divide salad among bowls; serve topped with tofu, nori and sesame seeds.

PREP + COOK TIME 30 minutes **SERVES** 4

HIGH IN
PROTEIN

SUPER
SPEEDY

TOFU LARB WITH CRISP RICE PAPERS

- 250g (8oz) firm tofu
- 4 green onions (scallions)
- ⅓ cup (80ml) lime juice
- ¼ cup (60ml) vegetable stock
- 2 tbsp soy sauce
- 1½ tbsp brown sugar
- 2 tbsp vegetable oil
- 1 long red chilli, seeded, chopped finely
- 1 stalk lemongrass, white part only, sliced thinly
- 1 tbsp finely chopped fresh ginger
- 1 cup (100g) coarsely chopped roasted walnuts
- 2 tbsp finely chopped coriander (cilantro)
- 1 gem (romaine) lettuce (180g), leaves separated
- 1 long red chilli, extra, sliced thinly
- lime wedges, to serve (optional)

CRISP RICE PAPERS

- ⅓ cup (80ml) vegetable oil
- 8 x 16cm (6½in) rice paper rounds

1 Pat tofu dry with paper towel. Crumble tofu into small chunks. Thinly slice white part of green onions. Shred green tops; reserve to serve.

2 Place lime juice, stock, soy sauce and sugar in a small jug; stir until sugar dissolves. Pour half the sauce mixture into a small dipping bowl; reserve to serve.

3 Heat oil in a large wok or frying pan over high heat; stir-fry tofu for 8 minutes or until golden. Add white part of green onion, the chopped chilli, lemongrass and ginger; stir-fry for 1 minute or until fragrant. Add the walnuts; stir-fry for 30 seconds. Add sauce mixture to wok; bring to a simmer, cook for 2 minutes or until reduced by half. Stir in coriander. Keep warm.

4 Just before serving, to make crisp rice papers, heat oil in a medium frying pan over medium-high heat. Cook one rice paper at a time for 30 seconds or until puffed. Drain on paper towel.

5 Serve larb in lettuce leaves, topped with reserved green onion and extra sliced chilli. Serve with crisp rice papers, reserved sauce and lime wedges.

PREP + COOK TIME 30 minutes **SERVES** 4

LOADED TOFU BURGER

200g (6½oz) five-spice firm tofu, grated coarsely
4 green onions (scallions), chopped finely
2 cups (150g) panko (japanese) breadcrumbs
1 cup (150g) plain (all-purpose) flour
⅔ cup (200g) vegan mayonnaise
4 vegan brioche burger buns (100g), split
1 cup (250ml) vegetable oil
1 baby fennel bulb (130g), sliced thinly
¼ cup (75g) vegan mayonnaise, extra
⅓ cup (110g) spicy tomato chutney
8 butter (boston) lettuce leaves (50g)
250g (8oz) vacuum-packed cooked beetroot, sliced
1 medium avocado (250g), sliced

1 Place tofu, green onion, 1 cup of the breadcrumbs, ⅓ cup of the flour and half the vegan mayonnaise in a large bowl; mix to combine.

2 Place remaining breadcrumbs and flour in separate shallow bowls. Combine remaining vegan mayonnaise with 1 tablespoon water in a third shallow bowl.

3 Shape tofu mixture into 4 equal patties. Dust tofu patties in flour; shake off excess. Coat patties in vegan mayonnaise mixture, then coat evenly with breadcrumbs. Place on a tray; refrigerate for 30 minutes.

4 Preheat oven grill (broiler) to high. Place split buns, cut-side up, on an oven tray; grill for 5 minutes or until toasted lightly.

5 Meanwhile, heat oil in a medium frying pan over medium heat (the oil is sufficiently hot when a sprinkle of breadcrumbs sizzles on contact). Cook patties for 2½ minutes each side or until golden and heated through. Drain on paper towel.

6 Combine fennel and extra mayonnaise in a bowl.

7 To serve, spread some of the tomato chutney on bun bases; top each with 2 lettuce leaves, fennel mixture, tofu patty, beetroot, avocado and a little more chutney. Season with pepper, then sandwich with bun top.

PREP + COOK TIME 25 minutes (+ refrigeration)
SERVES 4

SALT & PEPPER TOFU GREEN VEG STIR-FRY

- 600g (1¼lb) medium tofu
- ½ cup (150g) vegan mayonnaise
- ⅓ cup (60g) rice flour
- 2 tbsp white sesame seeds, plus extra, toasted, to serve
- 1 tbsp ground white pepper
- 2 tsp freshly ground black pepper
- 2 tsp sea salt
- vegetable oil, for shallow-frying, plus 1 tbsp extra
- 2 cloves garlic, crushed
- 2 tsp finely grated fresh ginger
- 1 tsp cornflour (cornstarch)
- ⅓ cup (80ml) soy sauce
- 200g (6½oz) sugar snap peas, trimmed
- 170g (5½oz) asparagus, trimmed, halved lengthways
- ½ small wombok (napa cabbage) (350g), shredded
- ⅓ cup (80ml) vegetarian oyster sauce
- 2 tbsp mirin

1 Place tofu on a plate lined with paper towel; top with another piece of paper towel and another plate. Stand, tilted, for 10 minutes to drain. Cut tofu into 2cm (¾in) thick triangles; pat dry with paper towel.

2 Meanwhile, mix vegan mayonnaise with 1 tablespoon water in a shallow bowl. Combine rice flour, sesame seeds, peppers and salt in another shallow bowl. Lightly coat tofu in vegan mayonnaise mixture, then coat in rice flour mixture.

3 Heat 1.5cm (¾in) vegetable oil in a heavy-based non-stick frying pan over medium heat. Shallow-fry tofu, in batches, for 2 minutes on each side or until golden. Drain tofu on paper towel.

4 Heat the extra oil in a wok over high heat; stir-fry garlic and ginger for 1 minute or until fragrant. Add the combined cornflour and soy sauce to wok with remaining ingredients; stir-fry until sauce boils and thickens slightly and vegetables are tender but still crisp. Remove wok from heat.

5 Serve vegetable stir-fry topped with salt and pepper tofu; sprinkle with extra sesame seeds and drizzle with a little of the cooking liquid.

PREP + COOK TIME 40 minutes (+ standing) **SERVES** 4

SERVING Serve with steamed brown rice and baby spinach.

TOFU & MUSHROOM TACOS

300g (9½oz) firm tofu, drained
3 large portobello mushrooms (600g), chopped
200g (6½oz) swiss brown mushrooms, halved
200g (6½oz) small button mushrooms
1¼ cups (320g) black bean and chipotle salsa
½ bunch coriander (cilantro), leaves reserved, stems and roots chopped finely
2 tbsp extra virgin olive oil
1 trimmed corn cob (250g)
8 small white corn tortillas (200g)
250g (8oz) non-dairy sour cream
1 large avocado (320g)
120g (4oz) cherry tomatoes, quartered

1 Crumble tofu into a large bowl, forming a mixture of large and small chunks. Add mushrooms, salsa and 2 tablespoons chopped coriander stems and roots; stir well to combine.

2 Heat 1 tablespoon olive oil in a large, heavy-based non-stick frying pan over high heat. Add half the mushroom mixture; cook, stirring occasionally, for 8 minutes or until mushrooms are browned and tender. Transfer to a bowl. Repeat with the remaining oil and mushroom mixture. Cut kernels from corn cob. Return all mushrooms to pan with corn; stir to combine. Season. Remove pan from heat; cover to keep warm.

3 Meanwhile, heat a chargrill pan over medium heat; cook tortillas, one at a time, for 30 seconds each side or until char marks appear. Transfer to a plate; keep warm.

4 Process non-dairy sour cream and the avocado until smooth. Season to taste.

5 Stir ½ cup coriander leaves through mushroom mixture; divide among tortillas. Top with tomatoes and remaining coriander leaves. Serve tacos with the avocado cream, drizzled with a little extra oil, if you like.

PREP + COOK TIME 40 minutes **SERVES** 4

TIP If you like things spicy, add a pinch of chilli flakes or sliced fresh chilli to the mushroom mixture.

SUPER SPEEDY

WARM GADO GADO SALAD

- 2 trimmed corn cobs (500g), each cut into quarters
- ½ small green cabbage (600g), cut into wedges
- 2 small orange sweet potatoes (500g), cut into 1cm (½in) slices
- 1 large zucchini (150g), halved lengthways, sliced thickly
- 1 medium red capsicum (bell pepper) (200g), sliced
- 200g (6½oz) sugar snap peas, trimmed
- 1 cup (80g) bean sprouts
- 1 long red chilli, sliced thinly
- ¼ cup (35g) roasted peanuts
- 2 tbsp sesame seeds, toasted

PEANUT SAUCE

- ½ cup (140g) smooth peanut butter
- ½ cup (125ml) coconut milk
- 2 tbsp light soy sauce
- 1 clove garlic, crushed
- 1 long red chilli, seeded, chopped finely

1 Line two large bamboo steamer baskets with baking paper; pierce holes in paper.

2 Place one steamer basket over a wok of simmering water. Add corn, cabbage and sweet potato to basket; cover with lid, steam for 5 minutes. Remove lid, add zucchini and capsicum to second steamer; place on top of basket in wok. Cover top basket with lid, steam for 5 minutes or until vegetables are almost tender. Add sugar snap peas to top basket; cover, steam for 2 minutes or until vegetables are just tender.

3 Meanwhile, to make peanut sauce, place ingredients in a small bowl with ¼ cup (60ml) water; whisk until combined. Season to taste.

4 Spread peanut sauce on a platter; top with vegetables. Sprinkle with sprouts, chilli, peanuts and sesame seeds.

PREP + COOK TIME 30 minutes **SERVES** 4

TIP Peanut dressing can be made a day ahead; keep covered in the fridge. Warm dressing before serving and add a little water if the consistency is too thick.

VEGAN CHEESE PARCEL & HAZELNUT SALAD

- 3 sheets fillo pastry
- ½ cup (125ml) extra virgin olive oil
- 200g (6½oz) vegan cheddar-style cheese
- 4 baby corella pears (400g)
- 1 cup (140g) hazelnuts
- ⅓ cup (80ml) maple syrup
- pinch sea salt flakes
- 2 tbsp wholegrain mustard
- ¼ cup (60ml) apple cider vinegar
- 2 shallots, chopped finely
- 1 medium radicchio (200g), cut into 1.5cm (¾in) steaks
- 1 medium fennel (300g), sliced thinly
- 1 bunch wild rocket (arugula) (120g)
- 1 bunch red dandelion (120g)
- 4 large purple figs (320g), halved or quartered

1 Preheat oven to 200°C/400°F. Line a large oven tray with baking paper.

2 Place one sheet of fillo pastry on a clean work surface; brush lightly with 1 teaspoon of the oil. Repeat layering with remaining pastry; brushing with 1 teaspoon of oil between each layer. Place vegan cheese in centre of fillo; carefully fold pastry over cheese to enclose. Place on lined tray; brush with 1 teaspoon of the oil.

3 Brush pears with 1 teaspoon of the oil. Place pears upright on tray with fillo parcel. Bake for 20 minutes.

4 Combine hazelnuts, 2 tablespoons maple syrup and sea salt flakes; toss to coat well. Remove tray from oven; scatter with hazelnut mixture. Return to oven; cook for a further 10 minutes or until pears are tender and pastry is golden and crisp.

5 Meanwhile, to make dressing, place remaining oil and maple syrup, the mustard, vinegar and shallots in a screw-top jar; season to taste. Shake well.

6 On a large platter arrange radicchio steaks, fennel, rocket, dandelion, figs, fillo parcel and quartered pears; drizzle over dressing. Scatter with the hazelnut crunch.

PREP + COOK TIME 45 minutes **SERVES** 4

GOOD
FOR GUT
HEALTH

NUT, SEED & TEMPEH FATTOUSH

300g (9½oz) tempeh, cut into 2cm (¾in) cubes
1 tbsp ground cumin
⅓ cup (80ml) extra virgin olive oil
1 tsp ground sumac
2 tbsp lemon juice
½ cup (140g) non-dairy yoghurt
1 baby cos (romaine) lettuce (130g), chopped coarsely
250g (8oz) cocktail truss tomatoes, sliced thickly
6 baby cucumbers (qukes) (180g), chopped
6 radishes (210g), sliced thinly
4 green onions (scallions), sliced thinly
1 cup flat-leaf parsley leaves
⅓ cup (55g) natural almonds, chopped
2 tbsp sunflower seeds, toasted
2 pieces wholemeal lebanese bread (115g), toasted, broken into pieces

1 Coat tempeh in cumin; season. Heat 1 tablespoon of the oil in a non-stick frying pan over medium heat; cook tempeh for 1 minute on each side.
2 Combine the sumac, 1 tablespoon lemon juice and remaining ¼ cup (60ml) oil in a small jug. Stir remaining lemon juice through the non-dairy yoghurt.
3 Place lettuce, tomatoes, cucumber, radishes, green onion, parsley, almonds and sunflower seeds in a large bowl with dressing, season to taste; toss to combine.
4 Just before serving, add toasted bread pieces and tempeh; toss gently to combine. Serve drizzled with yoghurt mixture.

PREP + COOK TIME 25 minutes **SERVES** 4

PAD THAI SALAD WITH CASHEW DRESSING

- 1 cup (150g) raw cashews
- ¼ cup (60ml) tamari
- 375g (12oz) rice stick noodles
- 1 medium carrot (120g)
- 200g (6½oz) daikon
- ½ medium red capsicum (bell pepper) (100g), sliced thinly
- 100g (3oz) snow peas, sliced thinly
- ¾ cup thai basil leaves
- 3 green onions (scallions), sliced thinly
- 1 long red chilli, sliced thinly

CASHEW DRESSING

- ½ cup (75g) raw cashews
- 2 tbsp tamari
- 2 tsp tahini
- 1 tsp maple syrup
- 3 tsp grated fresh ginger
- 1 tbsp lime juice
- ½ long red chilli, chopped finely

1 To make cashew dressing, place cashews in a small heatproof bowl with enough boiling water to cover. Stand for 10 minutes. Drain. Rinse under cold water; drain well. Blend soaked cashews with ¼ cup (60ml) water and remaining ingredients until smooth and creamy. Refrigerate until ready to serve.

2 Preheat oven to 160°C/325°F. Line an oven tray with baking paper.

3 Place cashews on lined tray; drizzle with the tamari, then toss to coat. Bake for 10 minutes or until cashews are dark golden.

4 Meanwhile, place rice stick noodles in a medium bowl; cover with hot tap water. Stand for 15 minutes or until softened; drain. Cool under cold running water; drain. Place noodles in a large bowl; add cashew dressing.

5 Cut carrot and daikon into julienne, using a julienne peeler, mandoline or V-slicer. Add to noodles with capsicum, snow peas and basil; toss to combine.

6 Serve salad immediately, topped with green onion, chilli and tamari cashews.

PREP + COOK TIME 30 minutes (+ standing) **SERVES** 4

FREEZE
ME

VEGAN MINCE & PUMPKIN SHEPHERDLESS PIE

- ¼ cup (60ml) extra virgin olive oil
- 400g (12½oz) plant-based mince
- 400g (12½oz) button mushrooms, trimmed
- 4 small cloves garlic, crushed
- 1 medium leek (350g), chopped finely
- 2 medium carrots (240g), chopped finely
- 2 tbsp tomato paste
- 2 tbsp plain (all-purpose) flour
- 2 cups (500ml) vegetable stock
- 1 tbsp vegan worcestershire sauce
- ⅓ cup tarragon leaves, chopped
- 700g (1½lb) kent pumpkin, peeled, chopped coarsely
- ¼ cup (60ml) non-dairy milk
- 2 tbsp pepitas (pumpkin seed kernels)
- 1 tbsp flat-leaf parsley leaves

1 Preheat oven to 200°C/400°F.

2 Heat 2 tablespoons of the oil in a large heavy-based ovenproof frying pan over high heat. Add plant-based mince; cook, stirring with a wooden spoon to break up any clumps, for 5 minutes. Transfer to a large heatproof bowl using a slotted spoon.

3 Add mushrooms and garlic to pan; cook for 5 minutes or until golden. Transfer mushroom mixture to bowl with plant-based mince using a slotted spoon. Add leek and carrot to pan; cook for 2 minutes or until softened. Add tomato paste; cook, stirring, for 1 minute. Stir in flour, stock, vegan worcestershire sauce and tarragon; bring to the boil. Reduce heat to medium; cook, stirring occasionally, for 20 minutes or until sauce thickens slightly. Return plant-based mince and mushroom mixture to pan.

4 Meanwhile, boil, steam or microwave the chopped pumpkin until tender; drain. Place in a bowl with non-dairy milk; mash until smooth. Season with pepper.

5 Spoon mashed pumpkin over plant-based mince mixture; lightly brush with the remaining oil. Transfer to the oven; cook for 40 minutes or until golden, adding pepitas for last 15 minutes of cooking time. Sprinkle with parsley.

PREP + COOK TIME 1 hour 30 minutes **SERVES** 4

MOROCCAN PLANT-BASED MINCE PILAF

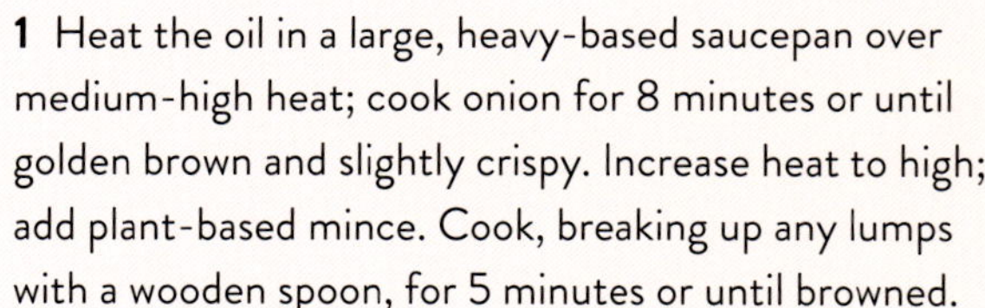

- 2 tbsp extra virgin olive oil
- 1 large onion (200g), sliced thinly
- 250g (8oz) plant-based mince
- 2 tbsp harissa seasoning
- ½ bunch coriander (cilantro), leaves reserved, stems chopped finely
- 1½ cups (240g) coarse burghul, rinsed well
- 400g (12½oz) can chickpeas (garbanzo beans), drained, rinsed
- 2 medium carrots (240g), julienned
- ¼ cup (20g) natural flaked almonds, toasted
- ⅓ cup (95g) non-dairy yoghurt

1 Heat the oil in a large, heavy-based saucepan over medium-high heat; cook onion for 8 minutes or until golden brown and slightly crispy. Increase heat to high; add plant-based mince. Cook, breaking up any lumps with a wooden spoon, for 5 minutes or until browned.

2 Add harissa seasoning and coriander stems; cook, stirring, for 1 minute or until fragrant. Add burghul; cook, stirring, for 1 minute or until toasted. Add the chickpeas and 1½ cups (375ml) water; bring to the boil. Reduce heat to low; cook, covered, for 15 minutes or until the liquid is absorbed. Remove from heat; stand, covered, for 5 minutes.

3 Fluff up grains with a fork. Top pilaf with carrot, reserved coriander leaves and the almonds. Serve with non-dairy yoghurt sprinkled with extra harissa seasoning, if you like.

PREP + COOK TIME 40 minutes **SERVES** 4

HIGH IN PROTEIN

VEGAN MINCE TACO SALAD

- 2 tsp olive oil, plus extra to serve
- 1 large red onion (300g), chopped finely
- 2 cloves garlic, chopped finely
- 500g (1lb) plant-based mince
- ⅓ cup (95g) tomato paste
- 30g (1oz) packet taco seasoning
- 400g (12½oz) can red kidney beans, drained, rinsed
- 175g (5½oz) plain corn chips
- 1 cup (120g) grated vegan mozzarella-style cheese
- 2 baby cos (romaine) lettuce (360g)
- 1 medium avocado (250g), sliced thinly
- 250g (8oz) cherry tomatoes, halved and quartered
- ½ cup coriander (cilantro) sprigs
- lime wedges, to serve

1 Heat oil in a large frying pan over high heat; cook the onion, garlic and plant-based mince, stirring, for 5 minutes or until plant-based mince is browned.

2 Add tomato paste, seasoning and 1½ cups (375ml) water to mince mixture; stir until well combined. Bring to the boil. Reduce heat to low; simmer for 10 minutes or until most of the liquid has evaporated. Add beans; stir until heated through.

3 Preheat oven grill (broiler) to high. Place corn chips, in a single layer, on an oven tray; top with vegan cheese. Place under grill for 2 minutes or until cheese has melted.

4 Meanwhile, separate outer leaves of lettuce; chop hearts coarsely.

5 Divide plant-based mince mixture and cheesy corn chips among bowls; top with lettuce, avocado, tomatoes and coriander. Drizzle with extra oil; season with pepper. Serve with lime wedges.

PREP + COOK TIME 35 minutes **SERVES** 4

FLAVOUR-ABSORBING MAGIC

MAGIC MUSHROOMS

MUSHROOMS Mushrooms have always aligned well with plant-based eating, in part due to a texture that can be made to mimic meat and a savoury or umami taste. Nutritionally they are a low calorie source of fibre, B vitamins and minerals. Their ability to carry flavour makes them a versatile ingredient with which to create magic in the kitchen with a range of uses, spanning everything from a pizza topping to moreish pie fillings.

MUSHROOM PIZZA WITH CAULI CRUST

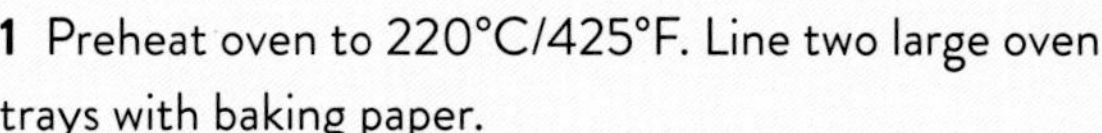

¾ cup (180g) non-dairy sour cream
2 tsp finely grated lemon rind
300g (9½oz) mixed mushrooms, sliced thinly
1 tbsp extra virgin olive oil
50g (1½oz) baby rocket (arugula) leaves
½ cup firmly packed basil leaves

OAT & CAULI PIZZA BASES

½ cup (80g) brazil nuts
½ cup (45g) rolled oats
500g (1lb) cauliflower florets
2 tbsp grated vegan parmesan-style cheese
3 tsp vegan egg replacer

ROCKET & BRAZIL NUT PESTO

¼ cup (40g) coarsely chopped brazil nuts
1 clove garlic, crushed
1 tsp finely grated lemon rind
1 tbsp lemon juice
50g (1½oz) baby rocket (arugula) leaves
1 cup firmly packed basil leaves
¼ cup (60ml) extra virgin olive oil

1 Preheat oven to 220°C/425°F. Line two large oven trays with baking paper.
2 To make oat and cauli pizza bases, process brazil nuts until coarsely chopped. Add rolled oats; process until finely chopped. Transfer mixture to a large bowl. Process cauliflower until very finely chopped. Add to oat mixture with vegan parmesan; season. Combine the vegan egg replacer with ⅓ cup (80ml) water in a small bowl; add to dry ingredients. Mix well to combine. Divide mixture between lined trays; press into 25cm (10in) rounds.
3 Bake pizza bases for 20 minutes or until light golden and dry to the touch.
4 Meanwhile, to make rocket and brazil nut pesto, blend or process ingredients with ¼ cup (60ml) water until smooth; season to taste.
5 Combine non-dairy sour cream, rind and 1 tablespoon water in a small bowl; season to taste. Spread mixture over bases. Drizzle each base with 2 tablespoons pesto. Top with mushrooms; drizzle with oil.
6 Return pizzas to oven for 12 minutes or until the mushrooms are golden and tender. Serve pizzas topped with rocket, basil and remaining pesto.

PREP + COOK TIME 45 minutes **SERVES** 4

GOOD FOR GUT HEALTH

MUSHROOM, TEMPEH & SOBA NOODLE STIR-FRY

- 270g (8½oz) dried soba noodles
- 300g (9½oz) spiced tempeh
- ¼ cup (60ml) extra virgin olive oil
- ½ tsp sea salt flakes
- 500g (1lb) mixed Asian-style mushrooms (see tip)
- 1 tbsp finely grated ginger
- 1 clove garlic, crushed
- 4 green onions (scallions), sliced thinly
- 1 long red chilli, seeded, chopped finely
- 1 medium red capsicum (bell pepper) (200g), sliced thinly
- 1 medium carrot (120g), julienned
- 170g (5½oz) asparagus, cut into thirds
- 100g (3oz) cavolo nero (tuscan kale), trimmed, shredded coarsely
- ¼ cup (60ml) tamari
- 2 tbsp lime juice
- 2 tsp sesame oil

1 Bring a large saucepan of water to the boil; cook the noodles for 3 minutes or until tender. Drain. Cool under cold running water; drain.

2 Pat tempeh dry with paper towel; cut into 5mm (¼in) thick slices. Heat 2 tablespoons olive oil in a large wok over medium-high heat; cook tempeh, in batches, for 2 minutes on each side or until golden and heated through. Drain on paper towel; sprinkle with salt flakes.

3 Heat remaining olive oil in wok over high heat; stir-fry mushrooms, ginger, garlic, green onion and half the chilli for 2 minutes or until just tender. Add the capsicum and carrot; stir-fry for 2 minutes. Add asparagus and cavolo nero; stir-fry for 1 minute or until tender.

4 Add noodles, tamari, lime juice and sesame oil; stir-fry for 1 minute or until heated through.

5 Serve stir-fry topped with tempeh and the remaining chopped chilli.

PREP + COOK TIME 25 minutes **SERVES** 4

TIP We used a mixture of king, shimeji, shiitake and oyster mushrooms. Slice larger mushrooms for even cooking.

MUSHROOM & CORN MISO RAMEN

- 2 x 300g (9½oz) packets medium or firm tofu, drained
- 1 cup (250ml) tamari
- 4 corn cobs (1.6kg)
- 2.5 litres (10 cups) vegetable stock
- 6 green onions (scallions)
- 40g (1½oz) vegan spread
- 3 tsp finely grated ginger
- ⅓ cup (80g) red miso paste
- 100g (3oz) shiitake mushrooms, trimmed
- 3 baby buk choy (450g), halved lengthways
- 180g (5½oz) vegan ramen noodles
- 1 cup (240g) frozen shelled edamame
- shichimi togarashi, to serve

1 Marinate tofu blocks in tamari for 1 hour. Drain; reserve 1 tablespoon tamari.

2 Remove husk and silks from 3 corn cobs; discard. Cut kernels from cleaned corn cobs; reserve kernels. Place the 3 trimmed cobs in a large saucepan with the stock. Trim 5cm (2in) off the top of the green onions; add tops to pan. Thinly slice remaining green onion.

3 Bring stock mixture to the boil. Reduce heat; simmer, covered, for 20 minutes. Strain stock mixture through a fine sieve into a large heatproof bowl; discard solids.

4 Meanwhile, heat vegan spread in a large saucepan over medium heat; cook reserved corn kernels, the ginger and two-thirds of the sliced green onion for 5 minutes or until tender. Add strained stock, miso, mushrooms and buk choy; bring to the boil. Add noodles and edamame; cook for 2 minutes or until noodles are just cooked. Stir in the reserved tamari.

5 Preheat a chargrill pan over high heat. Remove husk and silks from remaining corn cob; discard. Cook corn, turning, for 10 minutes or until char marks appear; remove from pan. Cook tofu blocks for 5 minutes each side; cut each block into six pieces. Cut kernels from cob in sections.

6 Ladle ramen into bowls; top with tofu, kernels and remaining sliced green onion. Sprinkle with togarashi.

PREP + COOK TIME 45 minutes (+ marinating)
SERVES 6

MUSHROOM PIES WITH SMASHED PEAS

- 100g (3oz) vegan spread
- 1 tbsp extra virgin olive oil
- 600g (1¼lb) mushroom cups, sliced
- 100g (3oz) shiitake mushrooms, sliced
- 1 bay leaf
- 1 medium leek (350g), chopped finely
- 1 clove garlic, chopped finely
- 2 tbsp plain (all-purpose) flour
- 2 tbsp tomato paste
- ¼ cup (60ml) vegan red wine
- ½ cup (125ml) vegetable stock
- 6 sheets frozen vegan shortcrust pastry, thawed
- 3 sheets frozen vegan puff pastry, thawed
- 2¼ cups (350g) shelled fresh or frozen peas

PREP + COOK TIME
1 hour 25 minutes (+ cooling)
MAKES 6

SERVING Top pies with vegan gravy, if you like. Most instant gravy is vegan.

1 Heat 60g (2oz) vegan spread and the oil in a frying pan over high heat. Add mushrooms and bay leaf; cook, stirring frequently, for 10 minutes or until mushrooms are soft and golden. Stir in the leek and garlic; cook for 2 minutes or until leek has softened.
2 Stir flour into mushroom mixture; cook for 1 minute or until vegetables are coated. Stir in tomato paste; cook for 1 minute. Add wine; stir until combined. Add stock, reduce heat to medium; cook, stirring continuously, for 3 minutes or until mixture boils and thickens. Cool. Discard bay leaf.
3 Preheat the oven to 180°C/350°F. Lightly oil six 10cm (4in) loose-based tart tins.
4 Cut a 20cm (8in) round from each sheet of shortcrust pastry. Line each tin with a pastry round; trim excess. Line pastry with foil; fill with dried beans or rice. Place tins on an oven tray. Bake for 20 minutes. Remove foil and beans; bake for a further 3 minutes or until pastry is golden and dry. Increase oven to 200°C/400°F.
5 Divide mushroom mixture among pie shells. Cut two 12cm (4¾in) rounds from each sheet of puff pastry; place a round on each pie, gently pressing the edge to seal. Cut a small cross in the centre of each pie.
6 Bake pies for 20 minutes or until pastry is golden and puffed.
7 Meanwhile, to make smashed peas, boil or microwave peas until tender; drain. Process hot peas with remaining 40g (1½oz) vegan spread until coarsely smashed. Season to taste with salt. Keep warm.
8 Serve hot pies topped with smashed peas.

MUSHROOM TOFU BURGER IN PUMPKIN 'BUN'

- 6 green onions (scallions)
- 300g (9½oz) extra firm tofu, chopped coarsely
- 200g (6½oz) button mushrooms, chopped coarsely
- 2 cloves garlic, crushed
- 2 tbsp dijon mustard
- 2 cups (200g) fresh wholegrain breadcrumbs
- 1 tsp vegan egg replacer
- 2kg (4lb) butternut pumpkin
- ¼ cup (60ml) extra virgin olive oil
- 4 slices vegan cheddar-style cheese (90g)
- 1 baby cos (romaine) lettuce (180g), leaves separated
- 1 large vine-ripened tomato (220g), sliced thinly
- ½ cup (160g) tomato chutney
- 1 tsp sesame seeds, toasted

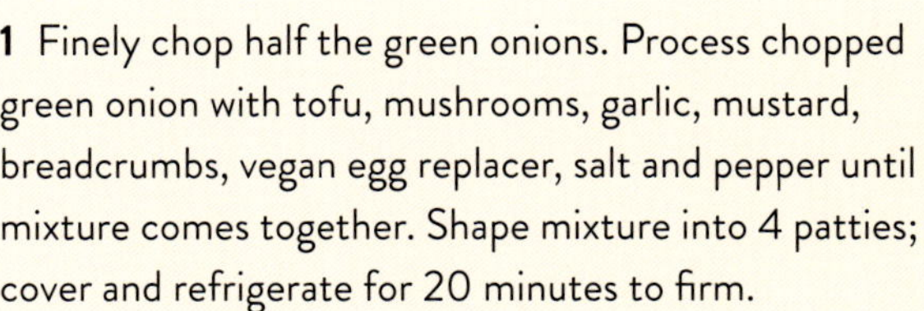

1 Finely chop half the green onions. Process chopped green onion with tofu, mushrooms, garlic, mustard, breadcrumbs, vegan egg replacer, salt and pepper until mixture comes together. Shape mixture into 4 patties; cover and refrigerate for 20 minutes to firm.

2 Meanwhile, cut unpeeled pumpkin in half widthways; reserve the stem end for another use. Cut the remaining pumpkin into eight 1cm (½in) thick rounds.

3 Heat 1 tablespoon of the oil in a large frying pan over medium heat; cook half the pumpkin slices for 5 minutes on each side or until golden and cooked through. Drain on paper towel. Repeat with another 1 tablespoon oil and remaining pumpkin slices.

4 Cut remaining green onion into 12cm (4¾in) lengths, then cut lengths into julienne. Place in a bowl of iced water to curl; drain before using.

5 Heat remaining oil in same pan over medium heat; cook patties for 2 minutes; turn over and cook for a further 1 minute. Top patties with vegan cheese and cook for a further minute or until golden and cheese is starting to melt.

6 To assemble, place a pumpkin round on each plate; top with lettuce, patty, tomato, chutney and curled green onion. Sandwich with remaining pumpkin slices; secure with short skewers. Sprinkle with sesame seeds.

PREP + COOK TIME 55 minutes **SERVES** 4

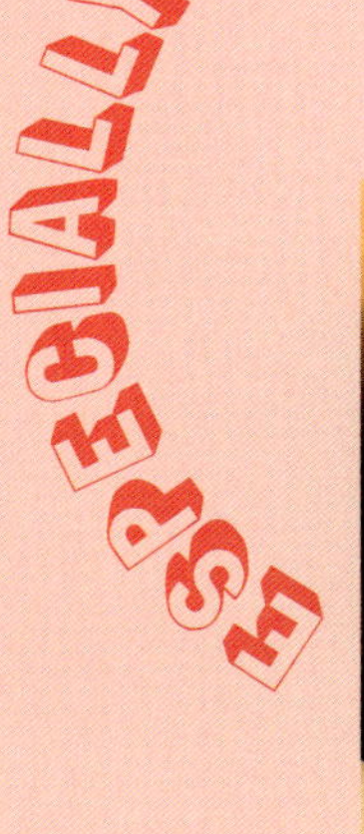
ESPECIALLY GOOD ROASTED

ORANGE VEGIES

SWEET POTATO • PUMPKIN These are carb-dense vegies packed with fibre and rich in carotenoids like beta-carotene which gives them their orange hue. Pumpkins have a relatively high water content that varies with type, so ensure you use the variety specified in the recipe. Sweet potatoes, like pumpkin, are rich in vitamin A and also contain fibres that promote gut health. Now let's get cooking with them!

SWEET POTATO & BLACK BEAN SAUSAGE ROLLS

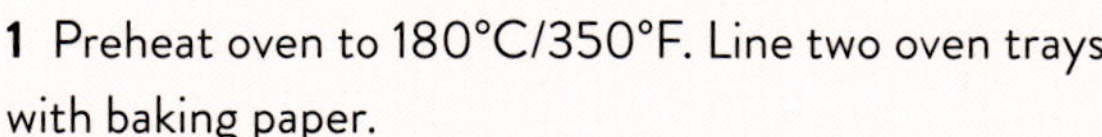

750g (1½lb) orange sweet potatoes, peeled, diced
1 medium red onion (170g), chopped finely
olive oil cooking spray
400g (12½oz) can black beans, drained, rinsed
⅓ cup chopped flat-leaf parsley
¼ cup (40g) pine nuts, toasted, chopped coarsely
100g (3oz) vegan fetta-style cheese, crumbled
1 tbsp non-dairy milk
2 tsp black sesame seeds
2 tsp white sesame seeds
1 cup (320g) tomato relish

VEGAN PASTRY

1 tbsp white chia seeds
2 cups (320g) wholemeal plain (all-purpose) flour
1 cup (150g) plain (all-purpose) flour
¾ cup (180ml) extra virgin olive oil
1 tsp sea salt flakes

PREP + COOK TIME 1 hour 15 minutes
MAKES 12

1 Preheat oven to 180°C/350°F. Line two oven trays with baking paper.

2 Place sweet potato and onion on one tray. Lightly spray with olive oil; season. Roast for 30 minutes or until potato is soft. Cool slightly. Increase oven to 230°C/450°F.

3 Meanwhile, to make vegan pastry, combine chia seeds and 2 tablespoons water in a bowl; stand for 3 minutes. Process flours, oil, ½ cup (125ml) water, chia mixture and salt until mixture just comes together (do not over mix). Transfer pastry to a clean work surface, bring together with your hands. Divide into four portions; wrap each in plastic wrap, refrigerate for 30 minutes.

4 Place roasted vegetables in a large bowl with beans; using a fork, crush lightly. Add parsley and pine nuts; mix well. Gently fold in crumbled vegan fetta.

5 Roll a portion of vegan pastry out on a lightly floured work surface until slightly larger than 18cm x 22cm (7¼in x 8¾in) and 4mm (¼in) thick; trim sides straight to rectangle measurements. Place a quarter of the filling mixture along one long edge; brush opposite edge with a little non-dairy milk. Roll to enclose filling. Cut roll into three pieces; place, seam-side down, on second lined tray. Repeat with remaining pastry and filling.

6 Brush top of rolls with remaining non-dairy milk; sprinkle with combined sesame seeds.

7 Bake the sausage rolls for 30 minutes or until golden brown. Serve hot or at room temperature with the relish.

GOOD FOR ENERGY

SUPER
SPEEDY

SWEET POTATO DHAL WITH CURRY SPRINKLES

1 tbsp coconut oil

2 small orange sweet potatoes (500g), grated coarsely

4 green onions (scallions), sliced thinly

1 clove garlic, crushed

2 tsp grated fresh ginger

2 tsp garam masala

1 tsp brown mustard seeds

400g (12½oz) can brown lentils, drained, rinsed

400g (12½oz) can diced tomatoes

1 cup (280g) non-dairy yoghurt

CURRY SPRINKLES

¼ cup (20g) shredded coconut

1 tbsp sunflower seeds

1 tbsp pepitas (pumpkin seed kernels)

1 tbsp raisins

2 tsp maple syrup

2 tbsp curry leaves

½ tsp ground cumin

½ tsp ground turmeric

¼ tsp curry powder

1 To make curry sprinkles, stir ingredients in a small non-stick frying pan over low heat for 4 minutes or until golden.

2 Heat coconut oil in a medium saucepan over high heat; cook sweet potato, green onion, garlic and ginger, stirring, for 3 minutes or until softened. Add the garam masala and mustard seeds; cook, stirring, for 30 seconds or until fragrant.

3 Add lentils, tomatoes and ½ cup (125ml) water to pan; bring to a simmer. Cook, stirring, for 5 minutes or until thick. Mash coarsely. Season to taste.

4 Serve sweet potato dhal topped with the non-dairy yoghurt and curry sprinkles.

PREP + COOK TIME 25 minutes **SERVES** 4

SERVING Serve with vegan indian flatbread or pappadums.

SWEET POTATO, BEETROOT & RICE PATTIES

- 300g (9½oz) orange sweet potatoes, peeled, chopped coarsely
- 1 large beetroot (beet) (200g), peeled, grated coarsely
- 125g (4oz) cooked brown rice
- ½ cup (45g) rolled oats
- ¼ cup (70g) tahini, plus 2 tsp extra
- 2 tbsp toasted sunflower seeds
- 1 tbsp ground cumin
- olive oil cooking spray
- 4 baby cucumbers (qukes) (120g)
- ⅓ cup (95g) non-dairy yoghurt
- 1 tbsp lemon juice
- 2 cups (20g) baby spinach leaves
- 150g (4½oz) cherry truss tomatoes, sliced
- 1 large avocado (320g), sliced
- lemon wedges, to serve

1 Preheat oven to 200°C/400°F. Line an oven tray with baking paper.

2 Cook sweet potatoes, covered, in the microwave on HIGH (100%) for 6 minutes. Place in a colander; stand for 8 minutes to cool and dry slightly.

3 Place the cooked sweet potato, half the beetroot, the rice, oats, tahini, seeds and cumin into the bowl of a food processor. Pulse a few times until coarsely combined but mixture comes together when pressed. Transfer to a bowl, stir through remaining beetroot; season. Shape mixture into four 8cm (3¼in) patties; place on lined tray and spray with oil.

4 Bake patties for 25 minutes or until golden at edges and cooked through.

5 Meanwhile, chop 1 cucumber. Place in food processor with non-dairy yoghurt, extra tahini and the lemon juice; process until smooth. Season to taste.

6 Slice remaining cucumbers thinly lengthways. Serve patties warm with spinach, tomatoes, avocado, cucumber and lemon wedges. Drizzle with yoghurt dressing.

PREP + COOK TIME 40 minutes (+ standing) **SERVES** 4

GOOD
TO GO

SUPER SPEEDY

SWEET POTATO & CHICKPEA CURRY

- 2 tbsp vegetable oil
- 2 cloves garlic, chopped
- 1 tbsp finely grated fresh ginger
- ¼ cup (75g) vegan thai red curry paste
- 1 medium orange sweet potato (400g), grated coarsely
- 270ml can coconut milk
- 2 cups (500ml) vegetable stock
- 200g (6½oz) firm tofu, diced
- 400g (12½oz) can chickpeas (garbanzo beans), drained, rinsed
- 100g (3oz) broccoli, cut into florets
- 1 medium red capsicum (bell pepper) (200g), chopped coarsely
- 120g (4oz) green beans, halved
- ⅓ cup coriander (cilantro) leaves
- steamed brown rice and lime wedges, to serve

1 Heat vegetable oil in a large saucepan over low heat; cook the garlic, ginger, curry paste and sweet potato, stirring, for 5 minutes or until sweet potato is tender. Stir in coconut milk and stock. Blend or process, in batches, until smooth.

2 Return curry to pan; bring to a simmer. Add tofu, chickpeas and vegetables; simmer for 5 minutes or until vegetables are just tender. Season to taste.

3 Serve curry topped with coriander; accompany with brown rice and lime wedges.

PREP + COOK TIME 30 minutes **SERVES** 4

BLACK BARLEY PILAF STUFFED SWEET POTATOES

- 6 medium orange sweet potatoes (1.8kg)
- ⅓ cup (80ml) extra virgin olive oil
- 1 medium onion (150g), chopped finely
- 1 tbsp ground cumin
- 1 cup (200g) black barley
- 2 cups (500ml) vegetable stock
- ¼ cup (35g) dried sweetened cranberries, chopped
- ½ cup coarsely chopped flat-leaf parsley
- ½ cup (90g) pistachios, chopped
- 125g (4oz) vegan fetta-style cheese, crumbled
- ⅓ cup flat-leaf parsley leaves

1 Preheat oven to 180°C/350°F. Line an oven tray with baking paper.

2 Scrub sweet potatoes; cut in half lengthways. Place potatoes, cut-side up, on tray; drizzle with 2 tablespoons of the oil and season. Bake for 1 hour or until tender.

3 Meanwhile, heat 1 tablespoon of the oil in a large saucepan over medium heat. Add onion; cook, stirring occasionally, for 5 minutes or until onion softens. Add cumin; stir for 30 seconds. Add barley; stir to combine. Add stock; bring to the boil. Reduce heat to low; cook, covered, for 40 minutes or until almost all the liquid is absorbed and barley is tender. Remove from heat; stir in cranberries and chopped parsley.

4 Remove the centre of sweet potatoes with a spoon, leaving a 1cm (½in) shell. Cut scooped flesh into pieces.

5 Spoon pilaf mixture into sweet potatoes, mounding it slightly. Top with sweet potato pieces, pistachios and vegan fetta. Bake for 10 minutes or until filling is heated through and fetta is light golden.

6 Serve topped with remaining oil and parsley leaves.

PREP + COOK TIME 1 hour 30 minutes **SERVES** 6

SWAP You can use regular barley or brown or black rice instead of the black barley, if you like.

FREEZE
ME

HARISSA & MAPLE PUMPKIN SOUP

- 2kg (4lb) kent pumpkin, peeled, chopped coarsely
- 1 tsp ground cinnamon
- ½ tsp freshly ground black pepper
- 2 tbsp extra virgin olive oil
- ½ cup (50g) pecan halves
- 1 tbsp maple syrup
- 1 large onion (300g), chopped coarsely
- 2 cloves garlic, sliced
- 2 tbsp harissa (see tip)
- 1½ cups (375ml) vegetable stock
- ½ cup (140g) non-dairy yoghurt
- ⅓ cup coriander (cilantro)
- chargrilled sourdough, to serve (optional)

1 Preheat oven to 200°C/400°F. Line a large oven tray and a small oven tray with baking paper.

2 Place pumpkin on large tray in a single layer; sprinkle with cinnamon and pepper, drizzle with half the olive oil. Roast for 25 minutes or until tender.

3 Meanwhile, place pecans on small tray; drizzle with maple syrup. Roast for 5 minutes or until golden. Cool.

4 Heat remaining olive oil in a large saucepan over medium heat; cook onion, garlic and harissa, stirring, for 5 minutes or until softened. Add roast pumpkin, stock and 1 litre (4 cups) water; bring to the boil. Remove from heat; cool for 10 minutes.

5 Blend or process pumpkin mixture until smooth. Return soup to pan over medium heat; stir until hot.

6 Ladle soup into bowls; top with non-dairy yoghurt, maple pecans and coriander. Season to taste. Serve with chargrilled sourdough.

PREP + COOK TIME 50 minutes (+ cooling) **SERVES** 4

TIP Harissa is a fiery North African spiced chilli paste. We use harissa sold in small jars that is less spicy than its counterpart sold in tubes. Adjust the amount of harissa according to which product you use and the heat level you prefer.

ROAST PUMPKIN & BROCCOLI WITH CHILLI DRESSING

1 small kent pumpkin (1kg), unpeeled, cut into thick wedges
2 heads broccoli (650g), cut into large florets
2 tbsp extra virgin olive oil
⅓ cup (15g) flaked coconut, roasted
⅓ cup (50g) raw cashews, roasted (see tips)
¼ cup thai basil leaves (see tips)

CHILLI DRESSING

2 tsp lime juice
2 tbsp tamari
2 tbsp brown sugar
2 tbsp peanut oil
1 long red chilli, chopped finely

1 Preheat oven to 220°C/425°F.
2 Place pumpkin and broccoli on a large oven tray; drizzle with oil, season. Bake for 30 minutes or until vegetables are browned and tender.
3 Meanwhile, to make chilli dressing, combine all ingredients in a small jug; season to taste.
4 To serve, arrange pumpkin and broccoli on a large platter; drizzle with dressing. Sprinkle with coconut, cashews and thai basil.

PREP + COOK TIME 40 minutes **SERVES** 4

TIPS To roast cashews, spread nuts on an oven tray. Roast in 180°C/350°F oven for 5 minutes, or until nuts are browned. Or, place nuts in a heavy-based frying pan; stir constantly over medium heat until browned. Use either method to roast flaked coconut, cooking for 3 minutes in oven. If thai basil is unavailable, use coriander (cilantro).

FREEZE
ME

PUMPKIN VEGIE BAKE WITH TAHINI SEED CRUMBLE

- 1 tbsp extra virgin olive oil
- 1 medium leek (350g), trimmed, white part chopped
- 1 tsp finely chopped rosemary leaves
- 1 tsp thyme leaves
- 400g (12½oz) can diced tomatoes
- 1 cup (250ml) vegetable stock
- 6 cloves garlic, peeled, bruised
- 2 medium carrots (240g)
- 3 medium parsnips (750g)
- ½ medium celeriac (celery root) (375g)
- 400g (12½oz) butternut pumpkin
- 2 celery stalks (300g)
- ½ cup (120g) non-dairy sour cream

TAHINI SEED CRUMBLE

- ¾ cup (115g) sunflower seeds
- ½ cup (60g) almond meal
- 2 tsp tahini
- ½ cup finely chopped flat-leaf parsley

1 Preheat oven to 200°C/400°F.

2 Heat oil in a medium frying pan over medium heat; cook leek and herbs, stirring, for 5 minutes or until golden. Add tomatoes, stock and garlic. Simmer for 10 minutes; season to taste.

3 Cut carrot, parsnip, celeriac, pumpkin and celery into 2cm (¾in) pieces. Place in a 21cm x 30cm (8½in x 12in) roasting pan; season with salt and pepper. Pour tomato mixture over vegetables; cover with a sheet of baking paper. Cover dish tightly with foil. Bake for 1 hour.

4 Meanwhile, to make tahini seed crumble, combine the sunflower seeds, almond meal, tahini and half the parsley in a medium bowl.

5 Remove foil and baking paper; sprinkle vegetables with seed crumble. Return to oven; bake, uncovered, for a further 15 minutes.

6 Serve vegetable bake topped with non-dairy sour cream and remaining parsley.

PREP + COOK TIME 1 hour 45 minutes **SERVES** 4

VEGETABLE TAGINE WITH ZA'ATAR CHICKPEAS

- 2 tsp extra virgin olive oil
- 1 large red onion (300g), chopped coarsely
- 2 cloves garlic, crushed
- 4 baby eggplant (240g), halved lengthways
- 500g (1lb) kent pumpkin, cut into 2cm (¾in) pieces
- 2 tsp each ground cumin, coriander and ginger
- ½ tsp ground cinnamon
- 400g (12½oz) can diced tomatoes
- 2 cups (500ml) vegetable stock
- 300g (9½oz) baby zucchini, trimmed, halved lengthways
- ¾ cup (200g) non-dairy yoghurt
- ½ cup finely chopped flat-leaf parsley, plus extra leaves, to serve

ZA'ATAR CHICKPEAS

- 400g (12½oz) can chickpeas (garbanzo beans), drained, rinsed
- 1 tbsp za'atar (see tips)
- 2 tbsp extra virgin olive oil

1 To make za'atar chickpeas, pat chickpeas dry with paper towel. Place in a medium bowl; toss with za'atar. Heat the oil in a small frying pan over medium heat; cook chickpea mixture, stirring, for 10 minutes or until golden.

2 Heat oil in a large heavy-based saucepan over medium heat; cook the onion and garlic, stirring, for 5 minutes. Add eggplant and pumpkin; cook for 1 minute on each side or until vegetables are browned lightly. Add spices; cook for 1 minute or until fragrant. Add tomatoes, stock and zucchini; bring to the boil. Reduce heat to low; simmer, covered, for 15 minutes or until vegetables are just tender.

3 Combine non-dairy yoghurt and chopped parsley in a small bowl; season to taste.

4 Serve tagine topped with yoghurt mixture, za'atar chickpeas and extra parsley leaves.

PREP + COOK TIME 1 hour **SERVES** 4

TIPS Za'atar is a Middle-Eastern spice mix; if you don't have any, make your own by combining 2 tsp dried thyme, 2 tsp sesame seeds, ½ tsp sumac and a pinch of sea salt. If you prefer, omit making the za'atar chickpeas and add the chickpeas directly to the tagine when adding the tomatoes in step 2.

LENTIL-TOPPED ROAST PUMPKIN

- 1.5kg (3lb) whole butternut pumpkin, scrubbed
- 2 tbsp extra virgin olive oil
- 2 large carrots (360g), cut into 4 pieces
- 4 shallots (100g), peeled
- 8 thyme sprigs
- 6 cloves garlic, unpeeled
- 1 cup (250ml) vegetable stock
- 400g (12½oz) can brown lentils, drained, rinsed
- ¼ cup (60ml) caramelised balsamic vinegar
- 120g (4oz) vegan fetta-style cheese, crumbled

1 Preheat oven to 200°C/400°F.

2 Cut pumpkin in half lengthways, cutting from base through to the stalk end. (Take care as the stalk end is particularly hard.) Using a metal spoon, remove and discard seeds. Make four widthway cuts, three-quarters of the way down into the flesh of each pumpkin, without reaching the skin.

3 Place pumpkin halves, cut-side up, in a deep roasting pan (see tip); season generously and drizzle with oil. Add carrot, shallots, 6 thyme sprigs and the garlic to pan. Pour over stock combined with ½ cup (125ml) water. Cover pan tightly with two layers of foil.

4 Bake for 45 minutes or until pumpkin is just tender (depending on the thickness of the pumpkin, it may require an additional 10 minutes). Remove pan from the oven. Uncover carefully, scatter over lentils; drizzle with balsamic vinegar.

5 Increase oven temperature to 220°C/425°F. Roast pumpkin and lentils, uncovered, for a further 15 minutes or until the pumpkin flesh is starting to brown and the braising liquid has reduced by half.

6 Serve lentil-topped pumpkin and roasted vegetables topped with vegan fetta and remaining thyme sprigs. Drizzle with a little of the braising liquid.

PREP + COOK TIME 1 hour 25 minutes **SERVES** 4

TIP Make sure the roasting pan is just large enough to fit ingredients. If it is too large, the liquid will evaporate too quickly.

GLOSSARY

ALLSPICE also known as pimento or jamaican pepper; is so-named because it tastes like a blend of nutmeg, cumin, cinnamon and clove – all spices.

BARLEY a nutritious grain used in soups and stews. Hulled barley, the least processed, is high in fibre. Pearl barley has had the husk removed then been steamed and polished so that only the 'pearl' of the original grain remains, much the same as white rice.

BAY LEAVES aromatic leaves from the bay tree available fresh or dried; adds a strong, slightly peppery flavour.

BEANS

black also called turtle beans or black kidney beans; an earthy-flavoured dried bean completely different from the better-known Chinese black beans (fermented soybeans). Used mostly in Mexican and South American cooking.

butter cans labelled butter beans are, in fact, cannellini beans. Confusingly, butter is also another name for lima beans, sold both dried and canned; a large beige bean having a mealy texture and mild taste.

kidney medium-size red bean, slightly floury in texture yet sweet in flavour; sold dried or canned.

BROCCOLINI a cross between broccoli and chinese kale, is milder and sweeter than broccoli. Each long stem is topped by a loose floret that closely resembles broccoli; from floret to stem, broccolini is completely edible.

BUCKWHEAT a herb in the same plant family as rhubarb; not a cereal so it is gluten-free. Available as flour; ground (cracked) into coarse, medium or fine granules (kasha) and used similarly to polenta; or groats, the whole kernel sold roasted as a cereal product.

CARAWAY SEEDS small, half-moon-shaped dried seed from a member of the parsley family; adds a sharp anise flavour when used in both sweet and savoury dishes.

CARDAMOM a spice native to India and used extensively in its cuisine; can be purchased in pod, seed or ground form. It has a distinctive aromatic, rich flavour.

CELERIAC (CELERY ROOT) tuberous root with brown skin and white flesh. When boiled and mashed, its flesh has the creaminess of potato, with a subtle celery flavour.

CHIA SEEDS contain protein and all the essential amino acids and a wealth of vitamins, minerals and antioxidants, as well as being fibre-rich.

CHICKPEAS (GARBANZO BEANS) an irregularly round, sandy-coloured legume. Firm texture even after cooking, a floury mouth-feel and robust nutty flavour; available canned or dried (reconstitute for several hours in cold water before use).

CHILLI

cayenne pepper dried, long, thin-fleshed, extremely hot, ground red chilli.

chipotle pronounced cheh-pote-lay. The name used for jalapeño chillies once they've been dried and smoked. Having a deep, intensely smoky flavour, rather than a searing heat, chipotles are dark brown, almost black in colour and wrinkled in appearance.

green any unripened chilli; also some particular varieties that are ripe when green, such as jalapeño, habanero, poblano or serrano.

long red available fresh and dried; a generic term used for any moderately hot, long, thin chilli (about 6cm-8cm long).

CLOVES dried flower buds of a tropical tree; can be used whole or in ground form. They have a strong scent and taste so should be used sparingly.

COCONUT

cream comes from the first pressing of the coconut flesh, without the addition of water. Look for coconut cream labelled as 100% coconut, without added emulsifiers.

milk not the liquid found inside the fruit (coconut water), but the diluted liquid from the second pressing of the white flesh of a mature coconut.

oil is extracted from the coconut flesh so you don't get any of the fibre, protein or carbohydrates present in the whole coconut. The best quality is virgin coconut oil, which is pressed from the dried coconut flesh and doesn't include the use of solvents or other refining processes.

CUMIN the dried seed of a plant related to the parsley family. Has a spicy, nutty flavour.

DAIKON a large radish with a crisp, juicy, white flesh, while the skin can be either creamy white or black. It has a sweet, fresh flavour, and is used in Japanese cooking.

EDAMAME (shelled soybeans) available frozen from Asian grocers and some supermarkets.

EGG REPLACER is available in the health food section of supermarkets and in health food stores.

FENNEL a roundish, bulbous vegetable with a mild licorice smell and taste. The bulb has a slightly sweet, anise flavour but the leaves have a much stronger taste. Also the name given to dried seeds having a licorice flavour.

GAI LAN green vegetable appreciated more for its stems than its coarse leaves.

GARAM MASALA a blend of spices that includes cloves, cardamom, cumin, cinnamon, coriander and fennel. Chilli and black pepper can also be added for heat.

GINGER

fresh also called green or root ginger; the thick gnarled root of a tropical plant. Keep peeled, covered with sherry in a jar and refrigerated, or frozen in an airtight container.

pickled pink or red coloured; available, packaged, from Asian grocers. Pickled paper-thin shavings of ginger in a mixture of vinegar, sugar and natural colouring.

HARISSA a Moroccan paste made from dried chillies, cumin, garlic, oil and caraway seeds. Available from Middle Eastern food shops and supermarkets.

JULIENNE PEELER looks like a wide-bladed vegetable peeler with a serrated blade and makes easy work of cutting vegetables into long matchstick-like strands; they are available from Asian grocers and kitchen stores.

KALE a type of leafy cabbage, rich in nutrients and vitamins. Leaf colours can range from green to violet.

LEEK a member of the onion family, the leek resembles a green onion but is much larger and more subtle in flavour. Tender baby or pencil leeks can be eaten whole with minimal cooking but adult leeks are usually trimmed of the green tops then chopped or sliced and cooked as an ingredient in stews, casseroles and soups.

LEMONGRASS a tall, clumping, lemon-smelling and tasting, sharp-edged grass. A very fibrous plant, so only the inner stem is used. Cut the stalks short and peel away the tough outer layers until you come to the more tender white part at the base.

LENTILS (red, brown, yellow) dried pulses often identified by and named after their colour. Eaten by cultures all over the world, most famously perhaps in the dhals of India.

LINSEEDS also known as flaxseeds, they are the richest plant source of omega 3 fats, which are essential for a healthy brain, heart, joints and immune system.

MAPLE SYRUP distilled from the sap of sugar maple trees found only in Canada and the USA. Maple-flavoured syrup or pancake syrup is not an adequate substitute.

MIRIN a Japanese champagne-coloured cooking wine, made of glutinous rice and alcohol.

MISO fermented soybean paste. There are many types of miso, each with its own aroma, flavour, colour and texture; it can be kept, airtight, for up to a year in the fridge. Generally, the darker the miso, the saltier the taste and denser the texture.

NORI a type of dried seaweed used as a flavouring, garnish or for sushi. Sold in thin sheets, plain or toasted (yaki-nori).

OIL

coconut see Coconut

olive made from ripened olives. Extra virgin and virgin are the first and second press, respectively, of the olives; "light" refers to taste not fat levels.

peanut pressed from ground peanuts; most commonly used oil in Asian cooking because of its high smoke point (capacity to handle high heat without burning).

sesame made from roasted, crushed, white sesame seeds; used as a flavouring rather than a cooking medium.

ONIONS

green also known as scallion or, incorrectly, shallot; is an immature onion picked before the bulb has formed, having a long edible bright-green stalk.

red also known as spanish, red spanish or bermuda onion; a large, sweet-flavoured, purple-red onion.

shallots also known as french shallots, golden shallots or eschalots; small, elongated, brown-skinned onions.

OYSTER SAUCE, VEGETARIAN while regular oyster sauce is made from oysters and their brine, vegetarian oyster sauce is made from mushrooms.

PAPRIKA ground, dried, sweet red capsicum (bell pepper); there are many grades and types available, including sweet, hot, mild and smoked.

PEPITAS (PUMPKIN SEED KERNELS) pale green kernels of dried pumpkin seeds; can be bought plain or salted.

POMEGRANATE MOLASSES not to be confused with pomegranate syrup or grenadine; pomegranate molasses is thicker, browner and more concentrated in flavour — tart and sharp, slightly sweet and fruity.

QUINOA pronounced keen-wa; is the seed of a leafy plant similar to spinach. It has a delicate, slightly nutty taste and chewy texture.

RADICCHIO a red-leafed Italian chicory with a refreshing bitter taste that's eaten raw or grilled. Comes in varieties named after their places of origin.

SAFFRON available ground or in strands; imparts a yellow-orange colour to food once infused. Quality can vary greatly; the best is the most expensive spice in the world.

STERILISING JARS it's important the jars be as clean as possible; make sure your hands, the preparation area, tea towels and cloths etc, are clean too. The aim is to finish sterilising the jars and lids at the same time the preserve is ready to be bottled; the hot preserve should be bottled into hot, dry clean jars. Jars that aren't sterilised properly can cause deterioration of the preserves during storage. Always start with cleaned washed jars and lids, then follow one of these methods:

(1) Put jars and lids through the hottest cycle of a dishwasher without using any detergent.

(2) Lie jars down in a boiler with the lids, cover them with cold water then cover the boiler with a lid. Bring the water to the boil over a high heat and boil the jars for 20 minutes.

(3) Stand the jars upright, without touching each other, on a wooden board on the lowest shelf in the oven. Turn the oven to the lowest possible temperature; leave jars to heat for 30 minutes.

Remove the jars from the oven or dishwasher with a towel, or from the boiling water with tongs and rubber-gloved hands; the water will evaporate from hot wet jars quickly. Stand jars upright and not touching on a wooden board, or a bench covered with a towel to protect and insulate the bench. Fill the jars as directed in the recipe; secure the lids tightly, holding jars firmly with a towel or an oven mitt. Leave at room temperature to cool before storing.

SUMAC a purple-red, astringent spice ground from berries growing on shrubs flourishing wild around the Mediterranean; adds a tart, lemony flavour to food.

TAHINI a rich, sesame-seed paste, used in most Middle-Eastern cuisines, especially Lebanese, in dips and sauces.

TAMARI a thick, dark soy sauce made mainly from soya beans, but without the wheat used in most standard soy sauces.

TAMARIND the tamarind tree produces clusters of hairy brown pods, each of which is filled with seeds and a viscous pulp, that are dried and pressed into the blocks of tamarind found in Asian grocers. Gives a sweet-sour, slightly astringent taste to marinades, pastes, sauces and dressings.

TAMARIND PUREE (CONCENTRATE) the distillation of tamarind pulp into a condensed, compacted paste. Thick and purple-black. Found in Asian grocers.

TEMPEH a traditional soy product from Indonesia. It is made by a natural culturing and controlled fermentation process that binds soybeans into a cake form.

TOFU also called bean curd; an off-white, custard-like product made from the "milk" of crushed soybeans.

firm made by compressing bean curd to remove most of the water. Good used in stir-fries as it can be tossed without disintegrating. Can also be flavoured, preserved in rice wine or brine.

silken not a type of tofu but reference to the manufacturing process of straining soybean liquid through silk; this denotes best quality.

TOMATO

paste triple-concentrated tomato puree used to flavour soups, stews, sauces and casseroles.

sun-dried tomato pieces that have been dried with salt; this dehydrates the tomato and concentrates the flavour.

truss small vine-ripened tomatoes with vine still attached.

TURMERIC also called kamin; is a rhizome related to galangal and ginger. Must be grated or pounded to release its acrid aroma and pungent flavour. Known for the golden colour it imparts, fresh turmeric can be substituted with the more commonly found dried powder. When fresh turmeric is called for in a recipe, the dried powder can be substituted (proportions are 1 teaspoon of ground turmeric for every 20g of fresh turmeric). Be aware that fresh turmeric stains your hands and plastic utensils (chopping boards, spatulas, the bowl of a food processor).

VINEGAR

apple cider made from crushed fermented apples.

balsamic originally from Modena, Italy, there are now many balsamic vinegars on the market ranging in pungency and quality depending on how, and for how long, they have been aged.

CONVERSION CHART

MEASURES

One Australian metric measuring cup holds approximately 250ml; one Australian metric tablespoon holds 20ml; one Australian metric teaspoon holds 5ml. The difference between one country's measuring cups and another's is within a two- or three-teaspoon variance, and will not affect your cooking results. North America, New Zealand and the United Kingdom use a 15ml tablespoon.

All cup and spoon measurements are level. The most accurate way of measuring dry ingredients is to weigh them.

When measuring liquids, use a clear glass or plastic jug with the metric markings.

The imperial measurements used in these recipes are approximate only.

DRY MEASURES

metric	imperial
15g	½oz
30g	1oz
60g	2oz
90g	3oz
125g	4oz (¼lb)
155g	5oz
185g	6oz
220g	7oz
250g	8oz (½lb)
280g	9oz
315g	10oz
345g	11oz
375g	12oz (¾lb)
410g	13oz
440g	14oz
470g	15oz
500g	16oz (1lb)
750g	24oz (1½lb)
1kg	32oz (2lb)

OVEN TEMPERATURES

The oven temperatures in this book are for conventional ovens; if you have a fan-forced oven, decrease the temperature by 10-20 degrees.

	°C (Celsius)	°F (Fahrenheit)
Very slow	120	250
Slow	150	300
Moderately slow	160	325
Moderate	180	350
Moderately hot	200	400
Hot	220	425
Very hot	240	475

LIQUID MEASURES

metric	imperial
30ml	1 fluid oz
60ml	2 fluid oz
100ml	3 fluid oz
125ml	4 fluid oz
150ml	5 fluid oz
190ml	6 fluid oz
250ml	8 fluid oz
300ml	10 fluid oz
500ml	16 fluid oz
600ml	20 fluid oz
1000ml (1 litre)	1¾ pints

LENGTH MEASURES

metric	imperial
3mm	⅛in
6mm	¼in
1cm	½in
2cm	¾in
2.5cm	1in
5cm	2in
6cm	2½in
8cm	3in
10cm	4in
13cm	5in
15cm	6in
18cm	7in
20cm	8in
22cm	9in
25cm	10in
28cm	11in
30cm	12in (1ft)

INDEX

Published in 2021 by Are Media Books, Australia.
Are Media Books is a division of Are Media Pty Ltd.

ARE MEDIA

Chief executive officer Brendon Hill

ARE MEDIA BOOKS

Executive general manger Sarah-Belle Murphy
Group publisher Nicole Byers
Editorial & food director Sophia Young
Creative director Hannah Blackmore
Managing editor Stephanie Kistner
Art director Jeannel Cunanan
Designer Kelsie Walker
Junior editor Georgia Moore
Food editor Sophia Young
Head of operations David Scotto

Cover recipe Mushroom & corn miso ramen, page 130
Photographer John Paul Urizar
Stylist Kate Brown
Photochef Rebecca Lyall
Additional internal photography from Adobe Stock images, pages 4-8, 34, 58, 94, 124, 136

Printed in China
by 1010 Printing International

A catalogue record for this book is available from the National Library of Australia.
ISBN 978-1-92586-641-4

Published by Are Media Books,
a division of Are Media Pty Ltd,
54 Park St, Sydney; GPO Box 4088,
Sydney, NSW 2001, Australia
Ph +61 2 9282 8000
www.awwcookbooks.com.au

International rights enquiries
internationalrights@aremedia.com.au

Order books
phone 1300 322 007 (within Australia)
or order online at www.awwcookbooks.com.au

Recipe enquiries
recipeenquiries@aremedia.com.au

womensweeklyfood